JOSH McDOWELL

D0963147

THE

DAVINCI
CODE

A QUEST FOR ANSWERS

JOSH McDOWELL

THE
DaVINCI
CODE

A QUEST FOR ANSWERS

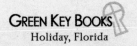

GREEN KEY BOOKS
Holiday, Florida

THE DA VINCI CODE: A Quest for Answers
Josh McDowell

©2006 by Josh D. McDowell. All Rights Reserved.

ISBN: 1932587802

Cover graphics: Kirk DouPonce, DogEared Design

Project management: JJ Graphics

Published by Green Key Books
2514 Aloha Place
Holiday, Florida 34691

Cataloging-in-Publication Data on file at the Library of Congress.

Printed in the United States of America

06 07 6 5 4 3

Acknowledgements

I want to thank the following people for their invaluable contribution to this work:

Bill Wilson for his researching expertise and completing the first draft;

Bob Hostetler for his winsome writing ability and crafting a story that wove the research throughout;

Dave Bellis, my resource development coordinator of twenty-nine years for guiding this project to completion;

Mike Duggins and Mike Sorgius for their vision and leadership in directing the entire national project of which this book is a part;

Brandon Hester for contributing substantial research to this book.

And finally to Green Key Books and Krissi Castor for the editing skills and vision to release this work.

— Josh McDowell

Disclaimer

Table of Contents

Preface:
A Journey of Discovery..ix

Chapter One:
"I Never Knew All That" 1

Chapter Two:
"I Have to Admit: I'm Hooked".............................11

Chapter Three:
"That's Pretty Persuasive" 35

Chapter Four:
"What Does That Tell You?" 59

Chapter Five:
"What Difference Does It Make?".......................79

Chapter Six:
A Quest Fulfilled 93

Bibliography...101

Preface
A Journey of Discovery

It is a phenomenon.

The success of the worldwide bestseller, *The Da Vinci Code*, took even its accomplished author by surprise. Dan Brown, already the successful author of the novels *Digital Fortress, Angels and Demons,* and *Deception Point,* nonetheless, confessed, "I never imagined so many people would be enjoying it this much."[1]

Since it was first released in 2003, Brown's book has sold more than thirty-six million copies and has been translated into forty-four languages...and counting.[2] It has spawned its own industry of sorts, including a special illustrated edition (with 160 illustrations interspersed with the text), guides on how to read the book, rebuttals, parodies, and an ABC television documentary.[3] Sony's Columbia Pictures paid six million dollars for the movie rights in 2003 and quickly lined up Ron Howard, Brian Grazer, and Akiva Goldsman (the Oscar-winning director/producer/writer trio responsible for *A Beautiful Mind*). Superstar Tom Hanks was cast in late 2004 to portray the lead character, Robert Langdon, opposite Audrey Tatou (*Amelie*) as cryptographer Sophie Neveu.

The plot of the novel revolves around the murder of the elderly curator of the Louvre, in Paris. Because the victim is surrounded with baffling clues and ciphers, Harvard symbologist Robert Langdon is called in to solve the riddle. Langdon's investigation unites him with French cryptologist, Sophie Neveu, and together they uncover the late curator's involvement in a secret society whose members included Leonardo da Vinci, among others. Their inquiry into a murder quickly becomes a quest to expose an ancient conspiracy and discover a shocking and priceless religious relic, suppressed for centuries.

In addition to explosive sales, *The Da Vinci Code* has ignited a resurgence of interest in Leonardo da Vinci, in particular, in Renaissance art, in general, and in books that explore historical topics and conspiracy theories, as well as a general interest in theories about Jesus, Mary Magdalene, and the early history of Christianity.

Around the world, those who have been fascinated by *The Da Vinci Code*—whether by the book, the movie, or both—are interested in delving deeper into artistic, historical, and spiritual mysteries. For many, Dan Brown's intriguing characters and conspiracies have opened new doors, posed new questions, and launched them on an exhilarating quest for answers. Millions of people want to know more about the secret societies mentioned in *The Da Vinci Code*. They're intrigued by the hints of mystery religions and evidences of "the sacred feminine" in the history of Christianity. They're hungry for more details about Jesus, Mary Magdalene, their relationship, and the Holy Grail. They're interested in all the twists and turns "the truth" took from the time of Jesus to the councils during the time of Emperor Constantine. And they would love to uncover layers of intrigue and conspiracy beyond those explored by Robert Langdon, Sophie Neveu, and Sir Leigh Teabing in Dan Brown's book.

That's what this book is about. As the subtitle suggests, it is a quest for answers, a further exploration of themes the novel introduced. And, like the novel, this book is itself a mere beginning, for the topics we will discuss in the coming pages can launch a lifelong journey of discovery.

The short upcoming chapters are structured as a series of conversations. The characters are fictional, but their discussions are based on real conversations, and the information they exchange is as real as the book you hold in your hands. For that reason, as much as possible, every claim that is made and every reference that is cited will be carefully noted. Extensive publishing information for every work that is cited is listed in a bibliography at the end of the book. The only exceptions to this format are references to *The Da Vinci Code*, which will be noted with page numbers only.

Though this book is designed primarily for those who have read *The Da Vinci Code* or seen the movie, a familiarity with the novel is not necessary to enjoy and profit from this small volume. Granted, there may be a few plot spoilers in the pages that follow, but the purpose of this book is to delve more deeply into the claims and conspiracies of the story, not to spoil the story for anyone. For those interested in further study, we have created a free, downloadable study guide to this book, available at josh.davinciquest.org.

So please join me on this journey of discovery, this quest for answers. Let's join the dialogue and dig deeper into the mysteries that have already proved so captivating to so many.

Preface Notes

1. From Dan Brown's website, quoted in BBC News interview, available at http:/news.bbc.co.uk/1/hi/entertainment/arts/3541342.stm.
2. See http://en.wikipedia.org.wiki/The Da Vinci Code.
3. "Jesus, Mary, and Da Vinci," originally aired on November 3, 2003.

Chapter One
"I Never Knew All That"

Chris held the door and waited for his friends, Matt and Andrea. The crowd of moviegoers filed through the door, and Chris started to wonder if he'd somehow missed them.

"There you are!" he said. "I thought I'd lost you."

Andrea rolled her eyes and elbowed her boyfriend. "He made me wait while he let everyone else go out in front of us."

Matt smiled sheepishly. "I was just being polite."

The trio fell in step with each other and exited the theater where they'd just watched the new *Da Vinci Code* movie together. Chris had known Matt and Andrea since freshman orientation last year at the university, having introduced them to each other while working at a registration table. They had been dating ever since.

"So," Chris said as they crossed the parking lot to the car, "what do you think?"

"About what?" Matt asked.

"He means the movie, Sweetie," Andrea said. "You know, the movie we just saw?"

"Oh," Matt said, punching the key fob to unlock the car doors. He cocked his head and opened the passenger door for Andrea. He spoke again after they were all in the car. "I don't know," he said. "I like Tom Hanks. He's a great actor."

Andrea turned sideways in the passenger seat. "I thought it was fascinating. I mean, I never knew all that."

"Like what?" Chris asked.

"Like the secret societies."

"Have you ever heard of them?" Matt asked. He pulled the car into traffic.

Chris shook his head. "Not really. At least not before reading the book."

"I think I need to read the book," Andrea said.

"You haven't read it?" Chris asked.

She shook her head.

"How about you?" Chris asked Matt.

He shook his head, too. "Nope. Everyone says it's really good, though."

"It's a page-turner, that's for sure," Chris said. "It's easy to read and hard to put down. So, why don't we read it, then? All three of us. We could meet once or twice a week and discuss it, over coffee. That would give us all a lot more to talk about than a two-hour movie."

"That's a great idea," Andrea said. "I mean, I'm really interested now in finding out more. This is all so new to me."

"Most of it's pretty new to me, too," Chris said. "What do you say, Matt?"

Matt nodded. "Well, I've got a pretty light load this semester," he answered. "So, as long as you're buying the coffee, Chris, I guess I'm in."

Andrea slapped her boyfriend on the shoulder. "You're so cheap, Matt."

The excitement begins

A week later, Matt and Andrea met Chris at The Daily Grind, their favorite coffee shop on one of the busiest streets in town; each of them held a copy of *The Da Vinci Code*.

"What do you think so far?" Chris asked his friends. They took a table by a window. To one side, a couple chatted under a Monet art print, and on the other side sat two college students playing chess.

"You're right," Matt said. "It is hard to put down."

"And there's a lot more detail on the conspiracy stuff," Andrea said. "And I think it's amazing to see this." She turned to the first pages of the novel, before the beginning of the story, and pointed to the words on page one:

FACT: *The Priory of Sion—a European secret society founded in 1099—is a real organization. In 1975 Paris's*

Bibliotheque Nationale discovered parchments known as Les Dossiers Secrets, identifying numerous members of the Priory of Sion, including Sir Isaac Newton, Botticelli, Victor Hugo, and Leonardo da Vinci.

The Vatican prelature known as Opus Dei is a deeply devout Catholic sect that has been the topic of recent controversy due to reports of brainwashing, coercion, and a dangerous practice known as "corporal mortification." Opus Dei has just completed construction of a $47 million National Headquarters at 243 Lexington Avenue in New York City.

All descriptions of artwork, architecture, documents, and secret rituals in this novel are accurate. [1]

"Yeah," Chris said, turning to that page in his own book. "Since our conversation in the car, I've done a little digging."

"What did you find out?"

What is Opus Dei?

"How about I start with Opus Dei?" Chris said. "It is a real organization within the Catholic Church."

"And is that true about its headquarters?" Andrea asked.

Chris nodded. "And people have accused the group of being, um, heavy-handed in their practices. Their critics say they brainwash and coerce and so on while others say that's not true. As far as I can tell, it's a very conservative group that attracts highly devoted people."

"I'd say," Andrea said, her tone scoffing, "that crazy monk is a highly devoted person!"

Chris smiled. "I think that character is the result of poetic license."

"What do you mean?" Matt asked.

"Every thriller needs a villain, and an albino monk from a shadowy organization is as good as any. But it turns out, though, *The Da Vinci Code* refers to him repeatedly as a 'monk.' There are no monks in Opus Dei."

"Really?" Andrea said. "Why would he do that? The author, I mean."

Chris shrugged. "Who knows? But in fact, Opus Dei's membership is almost all lay people; less than three percent are priests."

"But it's a pretty scary group, eh?" Matt asked.

"I don't know," Chris admitted. "Passionate, definitely. I'd say, if you're afraid of the Roman Catholic Church, you'd be very afraid of Opus Dei. But otherwise, no, I don't think it's scary. Except in the novel."

What is the Priory of Sion?

"Okay, what about the Priory of Sion?" Matt swallowed a swig of vanilla latte. "The book says some French king named Godefroi de-something-or-other started the Priory of Sion in 1099, right after he conquered Jerusalem. I'm a lot farther along in the book than Andrea is."

She rolled her eyes. "Until last night, maybe," she said. "But I've read that far now, too. King Godefroi was afraid the secret of the Holy Grail would be lost forever when he died, so that's why he started the Priory—to protect the secret and pass it on from generation to generation. And part of that had to do with finding and protecting the Documents—what were they called?"

"The Sangreal Documents," Matt interjected.

"Yeah, that's them," she said. "And it's so fascinating that the Priory still exists today."[2]

Chris nodded. "A little farther into the book, it talks about the proof of the Priory's existence being discovered in Paris's *Bibliotheque Nationale* in papers that came to be called *Les Dossiers Secrets*."

"No kidding," Andrea said. "That's fascinating."

Chris nodded slowly. "Well," he said, "that's where things started to get a little interesting."

"What do you mean?" Matt asked.

"Well," Chris said, "it looks like those documents really do exist, but they've been proven to be a fraud."

"What?" Matt said.

Chris shrugged. "Yeah, a historian named Paul Maier says *Les Dossiers Secrets* were planted in the *Bibliotheque Nationale* by Pierre Plantard. He says one of Plantard's co-conspirators admitted to helping him fabricate the documents, including the genealogical tables and lists of the Priory's grand masters—Newton, Botticelli, Leonardo, and so on."

"You're kidding," Andrea said.

"I'm just telling you what I've read. And it's not just one person saying this, either. It turns out that Plantard's hoax was exposed back in the nineties in a series of French books and a BBC documentary.[3] A New York Times reviewer revealed Plantard to be an anti-Semite with a criminal record for fraud while the real Priory of Sion is a little splinter social group founded just half a century ago."[4]

Andrea leaned back in her chair. "Are you sure? I mean, the book says it's a real organization, right there on page one!"

"Well, it is," Chris allowed. "It's just that instead of being founded in 1099, like in the book, the only documents that say it existed before 1956—when this Plantard guy registered it with the French government—have been exposed as hoaxes."[5]

"But it's a novel, right?" said Matt. "So he takes a few liberties to make a good story. That doesn't mean the whole thing is wrong."

Chris stood and pointed to their cups. "I'm going to get a refill. Anyone else?"

Andrea shook her head, but Matt agreed to another latte.

What is the Knights Templar?

When Chris returned a few moments later with the drinks, Andrea was ready.

"What about that other group, the Knights Templar?" she asked. "Are they a fraud, too?"

"No," Chris answered quickly.

"See?" Matt said.

"How far along in the book are you?" Chris asked.

Matt shrugged. "I'm somewhere around page one fifty or one sixty," he said.

Andrea opened to her bookmark. "One sixty-two," she said.

Chris quickly consulted his own copy. "Well, you're right there, then. It's on page one fifty-eight where Robert Langdon says the Priory of Sion created a military arm—'a group of nine knights called the Order of the Poor Knights of Christ and the Temple of Solomon . . . More commonly know as the Knights Templar.'"[6]

"So, wait a minute," Andrea said, her voice tinged with disappointment. "If the Priory of Sion never existed, they could never have created the Knights Templar."

"True," Chris said. "That part is fiction. But there actually was a group called the Knights Templar."

"There was?" Andrea said.

Chris nodded. "Yeah. The book says they went to Jerusalem under 'the guise' of protecting Christian pilgrims on the roadways of the Holy Land, but what they were really after was the Sangreal Documents, which they believed were hidden under the ruins of Herod's Temple. The book never says they found them but leaves the reader to suspect they did—and that they used these documents to basically blackmail the Vatican and achieve great wealth and power throughout Europe."

"Yes!" Matt said. "That's right where I am in the book." He flipped a few pages. "It says that Pope Clement V decided to take them out and 'seize their treasure' along with the secrets they held over the Vatican. He arranged with King Philippe IV for all the knights to be captured and burned at the stake, thus basically destroying the Knights Templar...though a few managed to escape." He paused for a moment and the others watched his eyes scanning the page. "It says the Pope wanted the documents but never got them because the knights had already given the documents to the Priory, which supposedly still has them to this day.[7]

"Is that true?" Matt asked.

"Well, yes and no," Chris said. He pulled out a single page of notebook paper from the back of his book. "Here's what I've found out so far. The Knights Templar were founded about A.D. 1118 by Hugh des Payens.[8] But I haven't found any evidence that the knights had any other mission than what all historians have said, more or less, until Dan Brown wrote this book."

"What mission was that?" Andrea asked.

"Protecting pilgrims to the Holy Land," Chris said.[9]

"That's not very exciting," Andrea said. She held up her copy of *The Da Vinci Code*. "I think I like this version better."

Chris smiled. "I hear ya," he said. "The knights did become wealthy, but it was through the gifts of pilgrims, not by blackmailing the church. And they eventually returned to Europe not because they had found some mysterious treasure, but because in the year 1291, all Christians were expelled from Jerusalem when the last Crusader fortress, which was located at Acre, fell to the Muslims."[10]

"So that's just more poetic license," Matt suggested. "A novel doesn't have to stick with the facts. Most novels are all made up, but this one at least has some facts in it."

"Yeah, but it's the conspiracy stuff that makes it so fascinating to me," Andrea said. "And it's starting to sound like most of the conspiracy is fiction."

Matt shrugged. "But it's good fiction," he said. "You're interested enough to keep reading, aren't you?"

"Yeah," she admitted. "But I almost think I'd rather not know which parts are real and which parts are pretend."

"Well, then," Chris said, "you don't want to know what I learned about the persecution of the Knights Templar."

"Maybe she doesn't," Matt said, "but I do."

Chris cast a quick glance at Andrea, who shrugged and stood. "I guess I will get a refill."

"Do you want me to wait until you get back?" Chris said.

"No, I won't be gone that long. Don't let me slow you down."

As she left the table, Chris turned over his page of notes. "I copied down a passage from one of the books I found. A historian from Oxford, England, named Karen Ralls quotes from *The Trials of the Templars Revisited*, which was written by Malcolm Barber, a professor of Medieval European History at the University of Reading. She says, 'The king did not proceed in the arrests of the Templars "through letters of the Pope."'[11] It was actually the other way around.

"These historians say it was King Philip who forced the pope to suppress the Knights Templar to get his hands on their money. The king—not the pope—arrested them and burned some, including Grand Master Jacques de Molay, at the stake in 1314.[12] One book I found said the pope was basically at the mercy of King Philip."[13]

Andrea had returned to the table while Chris was reading his notes to Matt. Chris paused only briefly before continuing. "It really sounds like Pope Clement tried to bend over backward for the Knights Templar as opposed to trying to destroy them to supposedly end their blackmail and get his hands on their mythical treasure."

Chris finished, and Matt and Andrea simultaneously sipped from their cups. Finally, Andrea spoke.

"You've done a lot of research," she said.

Chris shrugged. "Not really. This was all surprisingly easy to find."

"But," Matt said, "none of it's real proof. It's just that this book"—he tapped *The Da Vinci Code*—"says one thing, and these other people you're quoting say another."

Chris nodded and opened his mouth, but Andrea spoke first.

"Yeah, Sweetie, but the people Chris is quoting give footnotes and sources, and that sort of stuff, so you can check them out." She slapped her copy of the novel with an open hand. "This doesn't."

"Because it's a novel," Matt countered. "Some of it's true and some of it's not. Just like in those Anne Rice books you like so much, you think the descriptions of vampires are as factual as the descriptions of cities and streets?"

Chris looked on silently as his friends scrutinized each other's faces. Finally, Andrea sighed and leaned back in her chair. "Okay. Good point. But I want to know which is which. I want to know what's true and what's not."

"That's exactly the opposite of what you said a few minutes ago!" Matt said in a tone of exasperation.

She arched her eyebrows and pressed her lips together for a moment before saying, "I changed my mind."

Matt studied her for a moment, and then smiled admiringly. "Fair enough," he said. He looked at Chris. "The woman has changed her mind."

Chris smiled. "Well, all right, then," he said. "Let's just keep reading and get together again Thursday."

Chapter One Notes

1. 2
2. 113.
3. Hank Hanegraaff and Paul L. Maier. *The Da Vinci Code: Fact or Fiction?* (Wheaton, IL: Tyndale House Publishers, 2004), 12.
4. Laura Miller, "The Da Vinci Con," *The New York Times Book Review* (Sunday, February 22, 2004): 23.
5. See http://en.wikipedia.org/wiki/Priory of Sion.
6. 158.
7. 158-160.
8. Robert G. Clouse, "Templars," in *The New International Dictionary of The Christian Church*, gen. ed. J.D. Douglas (Grand Rapids, MI: Zondervan, 1974), 956.
9. Richard Abanes, *The Truth Behind the Da Vinci Code* (Eugene, OR: Harvest House Publishers, 2004), 57.
10. For facts stated in this paragraph, see William of Tyre, *Historia rerum in partibus transmarinis gestarum.* xii, 7; Addison, *The History of the Knights Templars, the Temple Church, and the Temple,* 3rd ed. (1852; reprint, New York: AMS Press, 1978); G.A. Campbell, *The Knights Templar: A New History* (Stroud, UK: Sutton, 2001); and Frank Sanello, *The Knights Templar: God's Warriors and the Devil's Bankers* (Lanham, MD: Taylor, 2003).
11. Malcolm Barber, "The Trial of the Templars Revisited" in *The Military Orders: Welfare and Warfare,* Helen Nicolson, ed. (Aldershot, England: Ashgate, 1998), 49; and Karen Ralls, *The Templars and the Grail* (Wheaton, IL: Theosophical Publishing House, 2003), 78.
12. Hanegraaff and Maier, *Fact or Fiction,* 23.
13. Abanes, *Truth Behind Da Vinci,* 60-61.

Chapter Two
"I Have to Admit: I'm Hooked"

Andrea sat on the couch in her tiny campus apartment. She was thoroughly engrossed in the story of Robert Langdon and Sophie Neveu, who were following a chain of cryptic clues and strange events to investigate a murder connected to a web of secret societies and the ancient search for the Holy Grail.

She turned page after page, watching Robert and Sophie peel back layer after layer of conspiracy, century after century of deceit. Desperately trying to stay one step ahead of the police, they were also managing to discover hidden codes and clues that the Roman Catholic church—among others—had worked hard to destroy.

Their knowledge was broadening and deepening considerably when they met Sir Leigh Teabing, a former British Royal Historian. "The Bible did not arrive by fax from heaven," Teabing says. Patiently and authoritatively, he tells the two detectives, "The Bible is a product of *man*, my dear. Not of God. The Bible did not fall magically from the clouds. Man created it as a historical record of tumultuous times, and it has evolved through countless translations, additions, and revisions. History has never had a definitive version of the book."[1]

Teabing's teacherly statements prompted Matt to open the discussion when he and Andrea met Chris at The Daily Grind that evening, taking their favorite table. "Andrea and I were up late talking about this guy Teabing in the book. It's amazing how much stuff I'd never heard before."

Chris stirred a packet of sugar into his cup. "Like what?"

"Well, like here," said Matt, "where he says the Bible is a product of *man*, not God. How man 'created it as a historical record of tumultuous times,' and how it evolved through the years."[2]

Chris sipped his coffee slowly. "Uh huh," he said.

"That part *was* fascinating," Andrea said.

Chris nodded and set his cup on the table.

"What?" Matt asked. "What's wrong?"

Chris shrugged and sighed. He seemed ready to speak several times but stopped.

"What is it?" Andrea asked.

Another sigh. "Well," Chris said. "That part bothered me."

"Why?" Matt asked.

"I don't know if you guys have read the Bible much," he started.

Matt looked at Andrea, and they exchanged smiles. "Not much," he said.

"Not at all," she answered. "I've never had much of an interest."

Chris nodded again. "Well, it's just that once Teabing started talking about the Bible, it was hard for me to stay involved in the story."

"Why?" Andrea asked.

"Well, I *have* read the Bible, and as soon as Teabing started saying those things, it was clear that he was no expert."

"What do you mean? He's a fictional character," Matt said.

"Yeah, but still, in order for me to suspend disbelief and buy into what's going on in the book, it's—well, distracting for a character who's speaking as an expert to be saying such uninformed things."

Matt's and Andrea's drinks sat untouched on the table. They both blinked at Chris as though he were speaking a different language.

"Okay," Chris said. "I'm not knocking the book because I really enjoyed it. But this speech of Teabing's was a real obstacle for me. It took me a few dozen pages to start enjoying it again."

"Because you disagreed with him?" Matt asked.

"No," Chris answered. "It was his ignorance of history."

"His ignorance?" Matt said. "He's supposed to be some famous historian."

"Exactly." Chris paused. "Okay," he said, opening the book to page two thirty-one, "he says men created the Bible 'as a historical record of tumultuous times.'"

"Yeah," Matt said. "So?"

What exactly is the Bible?

"Well, first, he seems to be totally ignorant that there are two major divisions of the Bible—the Hebrew Scriptures and what Christians call the New Testament."

Matt and Andrea stared blankly at their friend.

"Any historian who would try to speak with authority about the Bible would know that the Bible isn't at all like *this* book." He laid a hand on *The Da Vinci Code*. "This book was written by one man, over a relatively short period of time, and was published soon afterward.

"But historically speaking, the Bible is unique. It was written over a fifteen-hundred-year span by more than *forty* different authors from every walk of life. For example, Moses was a political leader trained in the universities of Egypt; David was a shepherd, poet, musician, and king; Joshua was a military general; Nehemiah was a palace official to a pagan king; Daniel was a prime minister; Luke was a physician and historian; and Paul was a rabbi, to name just a few.

"It was written in different places—in a desert, a dungeon, a palace, a prison, among others. It was written in three languages: Hebrew, Greek, and a couple short sections in Aramaic, the 'common language' of Jesus' day.[3] It was written on three different continents at different times, not just 'tumultuous times,' like Teabing says. For example, David wrote in times of war and sacrifice, Solomon wrote in days of peace and prosperity."

Chris reached for Matt's copy of the book which, unlike his own, was open to the page Chris referenced. "And maybe

what makes Teabing's statement most ridiculous, for a historian at least, is that he seems not to know it's much more than
'a historical record.' Sections of the Bible are history, but
other parts are poetry, proverbs, personal correspondence,
memoirs, satire, biography, autobiography, law, prophecy,
parable, and allegory."

"I didn't know all that," Andrea said. She turned to Matt.
"Did you?"

Matt shook his head. "No," he said. "But what's the
point?"

Chris took another sip of his drink. "My point is just that
it's hard for me to take seriously a character who's supposed to
be an accomplished historian and yet seems to be ignorant of
what the Bible is and how it came about."

Matt claimed his book back from Chris and focused his
gaze on the page. "So," he said, "when he says, 'History has
never had a definitive version' of the Bible, he's wrong?"[4]

Chris pursed his lips and thought for a moment. "It
depends on what you think 'definitive' means. And what you
think 'never' means."

When was the Bible 'collated'?

"What's *that* supposed to mean?" Andrea asked.

"Well, I hate to be picky, but think about what Teabing is
saying. First he says that history has never had a definitive version of the Bible, but then he says that the Bible, 'as we know
it today,' has been in the same form since the time of the
Roman emperor, Constantine—in other words, for the last seventeen hundred years. So which is it: never, or for supposedly
the last seventeen hundred years?"

"Wow, I see what you mean," Andrea said.

"I don't," Matt argued. "I think you're just being picky,
like you said. His point is that up until that time there was no
definitive version of the Bible."

Chris shrugged. "But that's not quite true, either."

"It's not?" Andrea asked.

Chris shook his head. "When it comes to the Old Testament, the evidence clearly supports the position that the Hebrew Scriptures—as we know them today—were collected and recognized long before Constantine, possibly as early as the fourth century B.C. and certainly no later than 150 B.C."

"Before Jesus?" Andrea asked.

Chris nodded. "Yes. The last books the Jews recognized overwhelmingly as authoritative—as being written by true prophets of God—were Malachi, which was written sometime around 450 to 430 B.C., and Chronicles, which was written no later than 400 B.C.[5] These books appear in the Greek translation of the Hebrew Scriptures, called the Septuagint, which was created between 250 and 150 B.C.[6] In other words, the books of the Old Testament were collected and translated into Greek not by the Vatican, not by the Emperor Constantine, not even by early Christians, but more than a hundred years before Jesus' birth as a result of the consensus of generations of Jewish rabbis and scholars. I'd say that's fairly definitive."

How many gospels were written?

"But it's not the Old Testament Teabing focuses on," Matt said. "He says there were more than eighty original gospels but only four were chosen.[7] And those were chosen for political purposes, to make people believe that Jesus was divine so they could 'use his influence to solidify their own power base.'"[8]

Chris nodded.

"Do you know anything about that?" Andrea asked.

Chris sighed. "About eighty gospels? No."

Andrea looked disappointed.

Chris opened his copy of *The Da Vinci Code* and pulled out a sheaf of papers. "I've known for years that there were so-called gospels that don't appear in copies of the Bible today. I could even have told you the names of some of them. *The Gospel of Thomas* is probably the most famous."

"So that's a real book?" Matt asked.

"Yes," Chris said.

"So that much is true, then," Matt said.

Chris nodded. "But there's no record of anywhere near eighty gospels as Teabing says." He leafed through the pages. When he found what he wanted, he laid the papers aside. "Before I read you this, though, let me ask you a question." He laid his hands palms up on the table. "If I laid on the table two different gospels and told you—" (indicating his left hand) — "one was written within a few decades of Jesus' life, and the other—" (indicating his right hand) —"was written a hundred or two hundred years later, which would you consider to be the most important, the most reliable?"

Andrea nodded and pointed to Chris's left hand. "That one," she said.

Chris lifted his left hand slightly. "The one that was written closest to the actual events?"

They nodded.

"Remember that," Chris said, "because that's going to be important." He picked up the pages and pointed to a circled excerpt. "Matt, would you read this?"

Matt took the pages from Chris and started reading:

There were not more than eighty gospel documents. For example, The Nag Hammadi Library, published in English in 1977, consisted of forty-five separate titles—

Andrea interrupted. "Wait a minute," she said. "That sounds familiar." She flipped the pages of her book and scanned a page and a half before she found it. "Here it is. Teabing mentions 'the Coptic Scrolls in 1945 at Nag Hammadi.'[9] I knew it sounded familiar."

"Yeah," Chris said, "Nag Hammadi is in Egypt, and it was a major discovery of ancient documents, the biggest until the Dead Sea Scrolls were discovered a few years later."

"He mentions those, too!" Andrea said, pointing to the page.

Chris shook his head slowly. "Yeah, which is really weird."

"Weird? Why?" she asked.

"Well, first because—what date does he give for the discovery of the Dead Sea Scrolls?"

She consulted the book. "He says they were found in the 1950s 'in a cave near Qumran in the Judean desert.'"[10]

Chris sighed. "For a character who's supposed to be a British Royal Historian, that's really weird.[11] History unequivocally records the discovery in the winter of 1946 or '47."[12]

"So he's off by a few years," Matt interjected.

"But that's not even the weirdest part," Chris added. "He says the Dead Sea Scrolls included some of the gospels Constantine supposedly tried to destroy, but there's not a single gospel in the Dead Sea Scrolls. They were the library of an ascetic Jewish group called the Essenes, not Christians."[13]

Andrea nodded, her brows knit together.

"Uh, excuse me, you two," Matt said, mock offense written on his face. "I was in the middle of reading something when you went skipping off on your little rabbit trails. I'll start at the beginning again." He read:

> There were not more than eighty gospel documents. For example, The Nag Hammadi Library, published in English in 1977, consisted of forty-five separate titles—and not all of them were gospels. In fact, it names five separate works as gospels: *Truth, Thomas, Philip, Egyptians,* and *Mary.* The collection of *The Gnostic Scriptures* by Bentley Layton has just short of forty works, three of which bear the title gospel and overlap with the Nag Hammadi list. In fact, most of these works were not gospels. The most generous count of extrabiblical documents appears in Harvard Professor Helmut Koester's *Introduction to the New Testament.* That count stands at sixty, excluding the

twenty-seven books in the New Testament. However, a vast majority of these works were not gospels.[14]

"Okay," Matt said, poring over the words he had just read. "So, let's suppose Teabing was way off. This still says there are at least five other gospels. It seems to me that's his main point."

"Yeah," Andrea agreed. "I never even knew that much."

"Have you ever read any of those?" Matt asked Chris.

Chris nodded. "A couple. They're not hard to find."

They looked at each other blankly until Matt broke the silence. "Well?" he said. "What do they say?"

"Are you sure you want to hear?"

"Why?" Andrea said. "What's that supposed to mean?"

"I don't want to spoil anything for you. I'm thinking it might be better to wait until we've all finished the book," he suggested.

"Oh, sure," Andrea said. "Like that's going to happen."

Matt spoke without smiling. "I'm starting to think you're enjoying this too much." He scooted his chair back. "I'm going to get another latte."

After Matt left the table, Chris turned to Andrea. "Is he upset?"

She rolled her eyes. "No. I think he's just getting impatient."

"Do you think he'll stop reading the book if I keep going?"

"No!" she said, quickly. "I don't think so. Besides, I'm really interested in what you're saying."

"Maybe I've been going about this all wrong."

"What do you mean?" she asked.

Just then, Matt returned to the table, and Chris started speaking before Matt sat down. "I've got an idea. Instead of me doing all the talking, why don't you guys swing by my house after we finish here, and I can loan you a few books so you can start researching some of these things with me?"

"That's a great idea!" Andrea said.

"Yeah," Matt agreed. "I like that. I like that a lot. It was getting to the point where I could see your lips moving, but all I was hearing was 'blah blah blah.'" He couldn't keep the corners of his mouth from turning into a sly smile.

"All right," Chris said. "This is going to be fun."

What do the other gospels say?

"You're in a lot of trouble," Andrea said as she and Matt met Chris at the door of the coffee shop for their next get-together.

"Why?" Chris asked as they wound their way through tables and chairs to their usual spot. "What did I do?"

"Neither of us has slept since you gave us those books," Matt complained.

"We have other things to do, you know," Andrea added, a mock rebuke in her voice. "Like my statistics course."

Chris had loaned a volume to each of his friends, urging them to compare Teabing's claims in *The Da Vinci Code* to what they read. He had assigned *The Infancy Gospel of Thomas* to Matt and a different document, *The Gospel of Thomas*, to Andrea.

After they had ordered their drinks and returned to the table, Matt spoke. "I've got questions, lots of them."

"Like what?" Chris asked.

Matt opened his copy of *The Da Vinci Code*. "This says that 'Constantine commissioned and financed a new Bible, which omitted those gospels that spoke of Christ's human traits and embellished those gospels that made Him godlike.'"[15]

Chris nodded. "Right."

"But it makes no sense if you read this," he said, opening the book Chris had loaned him to *The Gospel of Thomas*.

"Why is that?" Chris asked.

"Listen," Matt said. He started reading:

(1) When the boy Jesus was five years of age, and there had been a shower of rain, which was now over,

Jesus was playing with other Hebrew boys by a running stream; and the water running over the banks, stood in little lakes;

(2) But the water instantly became clear and useful again; he having smote them only by his word, they readily obeyed him.

(3) Then he took from the bank of the stream some soft clay, and formed out of it twelve sparrows; and there were other boys playing with him.

(4) But a certain Jew seeing the things which he was doing, namely his forming clay into the figures of sparrows on the sabbath day, went presently away, and told his father Joseph, and said,

(5) Behold, thy boy is playing by the river side, and has taken clay, and formed it into twelve sparrows, and profaneth the sabbath.

(6) Then Joseph came to the place where he was, and when he saw him, called to him, and said, Why doest thou that which it is not lawful to do on the sabbath day?

(7) Then Jesus clapping together the palms of his hand, called to the sparrows, and said to them: Go, fly away; and while ye live remember me.

(8) So the sparrows fled away, making a noise.[16]

"That's how it starts," Matt said.
Chris smiled. "Yeah," he said. "So?"
"If the whole idea was to promote the divinity of Jesus, you've got to wonder why this wasn't included in the New Testament!"

"Good point," Chris said.

"Hey," Andrea said, "at least the stuff you had to read made sense! I didn't understand half of what I had to read. It was just a collection of sayings, and most made no sense at all."

She read:

> Jesus said: Blessed is the lion which the man shall eat, and the lion become man; and cursed is the man whom the lion shall eat, and the lion become man.[17]

She read several other verses that left her companions shaking their heads in confusion. "What's that about?"

"Many scholars," Chris explained, "view *The Gospel of Thomas* as a Gnostic gospel. Gnosticism was a school of thought—actually, more than one school of thought—that sought salvation through secret knowledge. That may be why so much of *The Gospel of Thomas* seems cryptic. Do you think it reinforces what Teabing says in *The Da Vinci Code*?"

"I'm not sure," she answered. "If I remember right, didn't Teabing or Langdon say that the secret agenda of the church was to devalue women and exalt men?"

"Yeah," said Matt. "That was Langdon, back in the museum. Remember: 'so dark the con of man.' The church 'conned' the world by devaluing the feminine or something like that."[18]

"That's what I thought," Andrea said. "And Chris, didn't you tell me that this *Gospel of Thomas* was one of the Nag Hammadi documents Constantine supposedly wanted to destroy?"

"Yes, according to Teabing," Chris said, nodding.[19]

"Okay, then. So I'm reading along, and I get to the very end of *The Gospel of Thomas*, and here's what it says:

> Simon Peter said to them: Let Mary go forth from among us, for women are not worthy of the life. Jesus said: Behold, I shall lead her, that I may make her male, in order that she also may become a living spirit

21

like you males. For every woman who makes herself male shall enter into the kingdom of heaven.[20]

"So, I'm thinking the same thing Matt is," Andrea concluded. "If what Teabing says is true, *The Gospel of Thomas* seems to be the last thing some anti-feminine conspirator would try to suppress."

Chris agreed. "Especially since you won't find any statement even remotely like that in the New Testament itself."

Why were some gospels chosen, and not others?

Matt took a swallow from his coffee cup. "So, if documents like these weren't excluded as part of some grand conspiracy, why *were* they excluded? And why were the other ones *in*cluded?"

Chris paused. "Do you remember when I asked you which document you would trust more, the one written close to the events themselves or the one written much later?"

Matt and Andrea nodded.

"This is where your answer to that question becomes important. Because that's a large part of the reason the New Testament contains four Gospels and not five, or six, or eighty.

"You see, Teabing gives Robert and Sophie the impression that there were eighty different gospels circulating around that were on a basically equal historical footing with each other. He speaks as though the most important difference between these various gospels was whether they emphasized Jesus Christ's humanity or his divinity."

"Yeah," Andrea said. "And I'm not so sure about that claim any more."

"As a historian, though, Teabing really ought to know better," Chris continued. "There were far, far more critical considerations that went into certain books being accepted and others being rejected."

"Like whether the document was written soon after the events themselves," Matt announced as though he were in a classroom.

"Exactly," Chris said. "Now, it's going to take me a little time to explain all this. Should I take a break or keep going?"

Matt glanced at Andrea. She turned to Chris. "Keep going," she said.

"Okay. Let's start with one of the documents you just read. *The Gospel of Thomas.*"

"Wasn't Thomas one of Jesus' disciples?" Andrea asked.

Matt shot her a surprised look. "How do you know that? I thought you said you never read the Bible."

She shrugged. "I went to Sunday school when I was a kid."

"Thomas was one of the twelve disciples," Chris said, "but no one believes he was the real author of *The Gospel of Thomas.* Scholars generally consider it to have been written well into in the second century and *The Infancy Gospel of Thomas* around then or later.

"Similarly, *The Gospel of Philip* and *The Gospel of Mary*, which Teabing quotes from, can be dated no earlier than the second century, perhaps into the third century."[21]

"You mean, like, a hundred years after Jesus' lifetime?" Andrea asked.

"At least," Chris answered.

"By comparison, while there are differences between the opinions of conservative and liberal scholars, the evidence overwhelmingly confirms that the New Testament documents—including the four Gospels Teabing disparages—were of a very early date—especially compared to the so-called 'gospels' he quotes."

He flipped a page, laid the sheaf of papers on the table and turned it so Matt and Andrea could read it. "Here's a chart," he said, "that shows both conservative and liberal dating of the original writing of the books of the New Testament."

CONSERVATIVE DATING		
Paul's Letters	A.D. 50-66	(Hiebert)
Matthew	A.D. 70-80	(Harrison)
Mark	A.D. 50–60	(Harnak)
	A.D. 58–65	(T. W. Manson)
Luke	A.D. early 60s	(Harrison)
John	A.D. 80–100	(Harrison)

LIBERAL DATING		
Paul's Letters	A.D. 50–100	(Kümmel)
Matthew	A.D. 80–100	(Kümmel)
Mark	A.D. 70	(Kümmel)
Luke	A.D. 70–90	(Kümmel)
John	A.D. 170	(Baur)
	A.D. 90–100	(Kümmel)

(Figures on the chart above are from the following sources: Werner Georg Kümmel's Introduction to the New Testament, *translated by Howard Clark Kee, Abingdon Press, 1973; Everett Harrison's* Introduction to the New Testament, *William B. Eerdmans Publishing Co., 1971; D. Edmond Hiebert's* Introduction to the New Testament, Vol. II, *Moody Press, 1977; writings and lectures by T.W. Manson and F. C. Baur.)*

"Let me see if I understand this," Matt said, studying the chart carefully. "This says it's possible that the four Gospels that were included in the New Testament were written within forty or fifty years of Jesus' lifetime."[22]

Chris nodded. "The earliest as close as twenty years. And even some of those 'conservative' dates may not be conservative enough." He reclaimed the stapled pages and flipped another page. "For example, there was this guy named Irenaeus. He was Bishop of Lyons and probably the most important theologian of the second century. Oh, and as a young man, he sat under the teaching of Polycarp, who had been a disciple of John the Apostle, one of the Twelve. So Irenaeus was an important link to the apostolic age of the first century church.

"Anyway, he wrote this in a document called *Against Heresies* 3: 'Matthew published his Gospel among the Hebrews (i.e., Jews) in their own tongue, when Peter and Paul were preaching the gospel in Rome and founding the church there.'[23]

"Since historians know that Paul was in Rome from A.D. 60 to 64, Matthew probably finished his gospel at this time using notes and information he had collected over the years since he himself—Matthew, that is—walked with Jesus. As a tax collector, used to documenting data accurately, he was probably well suited for the task."

"So, to make a long story short, William Foxwell Albright, one of the world's foremost biblical archaeologists, said: 'We can already say emphatically that there is no longer any solid basis for dating any book of the New Testament after about A.D. 80.'[24] And the late Dr. John A. T. Robinson shocked the scholarly world when he announced his strong conviction that the whole of the New Testament was written before the fall of Jerusalem in A.D. 70."[25] He turned the page back to the chart and again positioned it before Matt and Andrea.

How was the New Testament assembled?

"So you're saying," Andrea said, "that the reason Constantine chose" —she quickly consulted the chart— "Matthew, Mark, Luke and John is because they were written so close to the events themselves?"

"No," Chris answered emphatically.

"No?" she echoed.

He smiled. "I'm saying Matthew, Mark, Luke, and John are in the Bible today partly because they were written so close to the events themselves."

"Isn't that what I said?"

Chris shook his head. "No, you said Constantine chose them. They weren't chosen and certainly not by Constantine."

"Whoa, wait a minute," Matt protested, crossing his arms and tipping his chair back on two legs. "I'm confused."

"I mentioned Irenaeus a few minutes ago," Chris explained. "By the time he wrote his book *Against Heresies*, a century-and-a-half *before* Constantine, those four Gospels were so universally recognized that he referred to them as four pillars, going so far as to say, 'It is not possible that the Gospels can be either more or fewer in number than they are.'[26] A few lines later, he says 'the Gospel is quadriform, meaning, of course, four in number.'"[27]

"In other words," Andrea said slowly, "more than a hundred years before Constantine, those four gospels were, like, pretty well accepted as...the...official ones?"

Chris once again reclaimed the sheaf of papers, prompting Matt to roll his eyes. Reading quickly, he said, "Let me read what the eminent Manchester scholar Dr. F. F. Bruce says on that point: 'It is evident that by A.D. 180 the idea of the fourfold Gospel had become so axiomatic throughout Christendom that it could be referred to as an established fact as obvious and inevitable and natural as the four cardinal points of the compass (as we call them) or the four winds.'"[28]

"But," Matt protested, "what about all those other gospels? Didn't they even consider them?"

"Some hadn't been written yet," Chris said, consulting the sheaf of papers again. "But about those that had, Origen, a prominent Christian scholar and theologian who died more than fifty years before Constantine became emperor, wrote:

> I know a certain gospel which is called 'The Gospel according to Thomas' and a 'Gospel according to Matthias,' and many others have we read—lest we should in any way be considered ignorant because of those who imagine they possess some knowledge if they are acquainted with these. Nevertheless, among all these we have approved *solely what the*

church has recognized, which is that only the four gospels should be accepted."[29]

"Wow," Andrea said, "that almost sounds like he'd been reading *The Da Vinci Code*!"

Chris laughed. "Let's just say that if Sir Leigh Teabing were a real person—and a real historian—he would certainly know that it was the early Christians who protected and passed on those writings which were genuinely from the apostles and who also warned against other writings which deceptively sought authenticity under an earlier disciple's name—like *The Gospel of Thomas* or *The Gospel of Philip*. In fact, history shows that well before Constantine, numerous writings and documents like the late-second-century *Gospel of Mary*, which Teabing quotes from, were considered false gospels by the overwhelming majority of Christians worldwide.[30]

Was the New Testament assembled to promote an agenda?

"See, in those early days, 'the church' was not an organization so much as an organism. It was not some well-established hierarchy of scholars and clerics in ivory towers and huge cathedrals. 'The church' was people like Origen's own father and many of his friends, who were put to death as martyrs because they refused to recant their faith in Christ. So when he talks about 'the church,' Origen is referring to that growing body of believers who recognized the writings of an apostle or someone who wrote under the authority of an apostle. Over time, there arose a broad consensus about which writings were trustworthy and which writings were spurious."

"So the councils had nothing to do with it?" Matt asked.

"No, but by the time the councils were finally convened, it was not for the purpose of selecting books. It was for the purpose of *verifying* which books the people of God had come to recognize as authentic... inspired, and that had been largely settled long before the first Council of Nicaea in A.D. 325. Contrary to what Teabing says, the debate at Nicaea con-

27

cerned not what books to include or even whether or not Christ was divine, but how to understand what those books said about Christ's deity.

"The evidence shows," Chris continued, pulling a small Bible from his hip pocket and propping his elbows on the table, "that even in the first century, Christians recognized certain contemporary documents as Scripture. Peter, just before his own death in A.D. 67, wrote of Paul's letters, saying, 'just as also our beloved brother Paul, according to the wisdom given him, wrote to you, as also in all his letters, speaking in them of these things...which the untaught and unstable distort, as they do also *the rest of the Scriptures*, to their own destruction.'[31] Did you catch that? By 'the rest of the Scriptures,' Peter meant the Old Testament. So it's clear that even before A.D. 70, followers of Christ had recognized certain New Testament books as Scripture on a par with the Old Testament.

"And after the apostles, other early church leaders recognized the same. For example, Polycarp (A.D. 115) and a later church leader named Clement of Alexandria (A.D. 150) referred to both Old and New Testament books with the phrase 'as it is said in these scriptures.'"

"Okaaay," Matt said. "But it seems to me that—even with all that, they still could have been 'stacking the deck,' the way Teabing suggests. You know, choosing only the books that promoted their specific agenda. He may have the details wrong, but there could still have been a conspiracy to achieve certain results."

Chris thought for a few moments. "I guess you could say there was an agenda, but that's not the same as saying they manipulated information."

Andrea arched her eyebrows. "Really. What was the agenda, then?"

Chris took his elbows off the table and leaned back in his chair. "There were good reasons why the church needed to recognize certain writings as authentically inspired and others as, um, spurious.

"First, I guess you could say their main agenda was formed by their belief that the writings of the prophets and apostles were truly and uniquely God's Word. It just follows that, if that is true, then clearly those writings should be recognized and preserved.[32]

"Second, the rise of heretics motivated early Christian believers to clearly define what had been recognized as inspired. In other words, not only should true writings be recognized and preserved, but pretenders and knockoffs, so to speak, had to be exposed and excluded. One early example was a man named Marcion who was born around A.D. 110. Sometime after A.D. 140, he developed his own theology and began to promote a list of accepted "Scriptures" (ignoring every book of the Old Testament and accepting only his revised version of the Gospel of Luke and eleven of Paul's letters). The church needed to counter his influence by collecting all the books of New Testament Scripture. In addition, some churches had begun to use books they did not realize were counterfeit, and church leaders began to recognize the importance of an agreed-upon 'canon,' meaning a standardized 'list' or 'index.'"[33]

Chris cleared his throat and took a sip of cold coffee with a grimace. "A third motivation was missions. As Christianity began spreading around the world and into new language groups that didn't understand Hebrew or Greek, it quickly became necessary to decide which documents should be translated and circulated to these new people groups.[34]

"And then, a fourth factor was persecution. The edict of Diocletian in A.D. 303 called for the destruction of the sacred books of the Christians—which, by the way, makes no sense if as Teabing says there was no definitive version of the Bible until the time of Constantine, twenty-three years later—"[35]

Andrea interrupted. "You're saying that an emperor twenty years before Constantine ordered the destruction of Christian Scriptures?"

Chris nodded.

"And everybody knows this?" Matt asked. "I mean, this is an established historical fact?"

"You can look it up," Chris said. [36]

"So," Andrea continued, "the Christians at that time kind of had to know for sure which books were truly—at least as far as their beliefs went—inspired by God, right? Because, who wants to die for a fake? Or even a nice book that's not necessarily sacred."

Chris smiled and nodded. "Exactly."

"So, before Constantine, it was pretty much decided," Andrea said.

"Pretty much," Chris agreed. "The majority of what we call the New Testament today was widely acknowledged a hundred years before Constantine. [37] Though it was not until A.D. 367, six years after Constantine died, that Athanasius (a bishop at Alexandria who was banished five times by various Roman Emperors) finally gave us the earliest list of New Testament books that is exactly like our present New Testament. [38]

"By the time a church council listed the twenty-seven books of the New Testament, it was a council called The Synod of Hippo in A.D. 393—it had nothing to do with deciding the canon but simply recorded the books that had been universally recognized by the church." [39]

Matt frowned and leaned over his copy of *The Da Vinci Code*, shaking his head. Chris and Andrea watched him, and for a few moments no one spoke.

"Something bothering you?" Andrea finally asked.

Matt lifted his gaze and looked from Andrea to Chris. His eyes narrowed. "That's just really disturbing."

"What is?" Andrea asked.

"Teabing says, as if it was unquestioned, that 'The Bible, as we know it today, was collated by the pagan Roman emperor Constantine the Great.'" [40]

"But you said it yourself, Matt," Andrea said. "It's a *novel*."

"But," Matt said, his agitation visible, "there's a difference between poetic license...and—and a poorly hidden agenda."

They sat silently for a few moments until Andrea broke the silence. "So are you saying you don't want to keep reading the book?"

Matt gripped *The Da Vinci Code* in both hands and lifted it from the table as if judging its weight. "No," he said. "I guess it's still worth reading if I want to find out what happens to the characters, right?"

Andrea seemed relieved. "I want to keep reading," she said. "Not just for the characters, though. I'm curious about more than just the Gospels and the Bible and stuff. I mean, Teabing may be wrong in that department, but maybe he and Robert and Sophie have a point in some other areas, you know?"

Chris grinned. "Sure," he said. "But I need to ask you guys if we can meet on campus the next time we get together."

They looked at him impassively. "Sure," Andrea said. "I don't see why not." She looked at Matt, who nodded in agreement.

"Good," Chris said. "There's someone I'd like you to meet."

Chapter Two Notes

1. 231.
2. Ibid, 231.
3. W.F. Albright, *The Archaeology of Palestine,* rev. ed. (Baltimore: Penguin Books, 1960), 218.
4. 231.
5. John F. Walvoord and Roy B. Zuck, eds., *The Bible Knowledge Commentary: Old Testament* (Wheaton, IL: Victor Books, 1985), 1573.
6. Norman L. Geisler and William E. Nix, *A General Introduction to the Bible* (Chicago: Moody Press, 1968), 24; David Ewert, *From Ancient Tablets to Modern Translations: A General Introduction to the Bible* (Grand Rapids: Zondervan, 1983), 104-108; and E. Würthwein, *The Text of the Old Testament: An Introduction to the Biblia Hebraica.* trans., Erroll F. Rhodes (Grand Rapids, MI: Eerdmans, 1979), 49-53.
7. 231.
8. 234.
9. Ibid.
10. 235.
11. 216.
12. Peter Flint and James Vanderkam, *The Meaning of the Dead Sea Scrolls: Their Significance for Understanding the Bible, Judaism, Jesus, and Christianity* (San Francisco: Harper SanFrancisco, 2002), 4.
13. Notwithstanding, the claims of authors Baigent and Leigh (whom Brown acknowledges in the very name of Sir Leigh Teabing—the last name being an anagram of Baigent) in their book, *The Dead Sea Scrolls Deception.* In this book, as well as in their previous *Holy Blood, Holy Grail* (from which Brown apparently draws the bulk of his "research"), the authors weave multiple conspiracy theories around the discovery and publication of the scrolls. However, the Baigent/Leigh book does not state (as Teabing does) that any of the "gospels" Constantine supposedly tried to destroy are found among the Dead Sea Scrolls. See Michael Baigent, *The Dead Sea Scrolls Deception* (New York: Simon & Schuster, 1991) and Michael Baigent, Richard Leigh, and Henry Lincoln, *Holy Blood, Holy Grail* (New York: Dell Publishing, 1982).
14. Darrell L. Bock, *Breaking the Da Vinci Code* (Nashville: Thomas Nelson, Publishers, 2004), 61-62.
15. 234.
16. "Infancy Gospel of Thomas, 1:2-9," in *The Lost Books of the Bible and the Forgotten Books of Eden* (Dallas: Word Publishing, 1994), 60.
17. Ibid, 7.
18. 1214.

19. 234.
20. "The Gospel of Thomas," 114.
21. 246-247.
22. For more extensive information on the dating of New Testament manuscripts and related issues, see *The New Evidence that Demands a Verdict* (Nashville: Thomas Nelson Publishers, 1999) by Josh McDowell.
23. Irenaeus, *Against Heresies,* in *The Ante-Nicene Fathers,* vol. 1, eds. James Donaldson and Alexander Roberts (Grand Rapids, MI: Eerdmans, 1993), 3.1.1.
24. W.F. Albright, *Recent Discoveries in Bible Lands* (New York: Funk and Wagnalls, 1955), 136.
25. John A.T. Robinson, *Redating the New Testament* (Philadelphia: Westminster, 1976).
26. Irenaeus, *Against Heresies*, 3.11.8.
27. Ibid.
28. F.F. Bruce, *The Books and the Parchments: How We Got Our English Bible* (Old Tappan, NJ: Fleming H. Revell, 1950), 109.
29. Darrell L. Bock, *Breaking the Da Vinci Code* (Nashville: Thomas Nelson, 2004), 119-120.
30. Eusebius, *The History of the Church,* trans. by G. A. Williamson (New York: Penguin Classics, 1989), 3.3-4, 24-25; 5.8; 6.14, 25.
31. 2 Peter 3:15, 16, NASB.
31. Professors Geisler and Nix state, "The initial reason for collecting and preserving the inspired books was that they were prophetic. That is, since they were written by an apostle or prophet of God, they must be valuable, and if valuable, they should be preserved. This reasoning is apparent in apostolic times by the collection and circulation of Paul's epistles (cf. 2 Peter 3:15-16; Col. 4:16)" in Norman L. Geisler and William E. Nix, *A General Introduction to the Bible* (Chicago: Moody Press, 1968), 277.
33. As applied to Scripture, *canon* means "an officially accepted list of books." Ralph Earle, *How We Got Our Bible* (Grand Rapids, MI: Baker Book House, 1971), 31; and Bruce, *Books and Parchments*, 95.
34. Dr. Norman Geisler writes, "Christianity had spread rapidly to other countries, and there was the need to translate the Bible into those other languages...As early as the first half of the second century the Bible was translated into Syriac and Old Latin. But because the missionaries could not translate a Bible that did not exist, attention was necessarily drawn to the question of which books really belonged to the authoritative Christian canon" in *General Introduction*, 278.
35. Everett Ferguson, "Factors Leading to the Selection and Closure of the New Testament Canon," in *The Canon Debate,* eds. Lee Martin McDonald and James A. Sanders (Peabody, MA: Hendrickson Publishers, 2002), 317.

36. Eusebius: *The History of the Church*, trans. by G. A. Williamson (New York: Penguin Classics, 1989); *Lactanticus: De Mortibus Persecutorum* (1984), trans. by J.L. Creed.

37. Former Yale Professor of Ecclesiastical History, Williston Walker, writes: "By about 200 A.D., according to the witness of the Muratorian fragment, Western Christendom had a New Testament canon embracing *Matthew, Mark, Luke, John, Acts, 1 and 2 Corinthians, Ephesians, Philippians, Colossians, Galatians, 1 and 2 Thessalonians, Romans, Philemon, Titus, 1 and 2 Timothy, Jude, 1 and 2 John, Revelation*, and the so-called *Apocalypse of Peter*." He concludes, "By the year 200 the church of the western portion of the empire had, therefore, an authoritative collection of New Testament books, in the main like our own, to which to appeal," in *A History of the Christian Church* (New York: Charles Scribner's Sons, 1970), 59-60.

38. Athanasius, *Letters,* no. 39 (Easter 367), in *A Select Library of the New Testament and Other Early Christian Literature* (Chicago: The University of Chicago Press, 1952), 552.

39. Bruce, *Books and Parchments*, 113.

40. 231.

Chapter Three
"That's Pretty Persuasive"

Chris, Matt, and Andrea entered the cramped university office of Dr. Maria Martinez. She greeted the trio warmly, her fluent English flavored with a hint of Spanish. They declined the hot tea she offered, so she fixed her own in a china cup and then settled behind her desk.

Chris thanked Dr. Martinez for her time and explained that they'd been reading *The Da Vinci Code* and had questions about it. He turned to Matt and Andrea. "Dr. Martinez is an accomplished historian of the early church and an expert on the church fathers."

"Church...fathers?" Andrea asked.

Dr. Martinez smiled. "The generation of leaders and writers who followed the age of the apostles," she said. "The church fathers were people like Justin Martyr, Irenaeus, Origen, and Tertullian, among others." She stirred her tea and looked from Andrea to Matt. "What can I do for you?"

Did Christianity win a power struggle with paganism?

Matt and Andrea turned, as if on cue, and looked expectantly at Chris. He smiled. "I'm not sure where to start," he said. "But one thing that surprised me when I first read *The Da Vinci Code* was its depiction of early church history as a kind of power struggle, internally and externally."

Dr. Martinez nodded slowly and sipped her tea. "Can you give me an example?"

Chris started to respond, but Matt, leaning forward in his chair and flipping open his copy of *The Da Vinci Code*, spoke first. "I think so," he said. "It says here, 'Christians and pagans began warring, and the conflict grew to such proportions that it threatened to rend Rome in two.'"[1]

"What pagans are we talking about?" Dr. Martinez asked.

Matt looked at her quizzically. "What do you mean?"

Dr. Martinez stirred her tea without touching the spoon to the sides of the cup. "There are many kinds of paganism," she said in her musical accent. "Pagan—at least in the first few centuries after Jesus' lifetime—meant simply someone who was not Jewish or Christian. So there were pagans who worshiped the Roman pantheon of gods, pagans who engaged in nature worship, pagans who worshiped unknown gods, as evidenced in Paul's visit to Athens.[2] And those are just a few examples. The non-Christian religions of the Mediterranean world were multiple and diverse and cannot be treated as a unified phenomenon."[3]

"Oh, I get it," Matt responded. He consulted the book. "It says here that before Christianity became the official religion of the Roman Empire—"

"I beg your pardon?" Dr. Martinez interrupted.

Matt looked momentarily like a deer caught in headlights. "I was saying that before Christianity became the official religion of the Roman Empire—"

"Are you saying that book says such a thing?"

He nodded and read to her. "It says, 'In A.D. 325, he decided to unify Rome under a single religion. Christianity.' And then Sophie—she's one of the characters in the book—she says, 'Why would a pagan emperor choose Christianity as the official religion?'"[4]

Dr. Martinez nodded seriously. "Fascinating. Artful, in fact." She leaned forward and clasped her hands in front of her. "The fact is, there was no 'official religion' of Rome, not even emperor worship, per se. The empire had a policy of mutual toleration, meaning all ancient religions and sects were tolerated as long as its adherents also tolerated all others. Christianity was not tolerated because its converts declared allegiance only to Jesus. And Constantine absolutely did not make Christianity the 'official religion' of anything; the Edict of Milan in the year A.D. 313 simply declared that Christian worship was to be tolerated, for the first time."[5]

"But," Matt said, "this says that 'in Constantine's day, Rome's official religion was sun worship.'"[6]

Dr. Martinez chuckled, shaking her head. "I hope his fiction is better than his history."

"So that's not true, either?" Andrea asked.

Martinez sighed. "Sun worship was practiced in Rome, but there was nothing like an official religion. And if there had been, it wouldn't have been sun worship."

Chris jumped into the conversation. "What about the impression the book gives that there was this great power struggle between Christianity and paganism, and Christianity basically won out?"

Andrea nodded. "Yeah," she said. "Is that true?"

Dr. Martinez took another sip of tea and set the cup in the saucer. "Yes and no," she said. "Remember, Christianity was a movement begun by a teacher who commanded love for one's enemies and said, 'My kingdom is not of this world.'[7] There were indeed great tensions between early Christianity and some forms of paganism and the more so because Christianity was an illegal religion until the Edict of Milan, but to say that 'Christians and pagans began warring' is an extremely inaccurate choice of words. Many of the early Christians were martyred for their faith, choosing death for themselves, not 'warring' against those who didn't share their faith. That's a demonstrably false impression."

"So," Chris interjected, "rather than a group of people all 'hung up' over competition from pagans..."

Dr. Martinez happily took the bait. "Christians were being hung up *by* pagans...literally."

Did Christianity really get its story from pagan religions and myths?

Andrea looked up shyly from her copy of *The Da Vinci Code*. "May I ask a question?"

"That is why we're here," Dr. Martinez said.

She flashed an embarrassed smile. "The historian in the story's name is Sir Leigh Teabing, and he says this:

> Nothing in Christianity is original. The pre-Christian God Mithras—called *the Son of God* and *the Light of the World* was born on December 25, died, was buried in a rock tomb, and then resurrected in three days. By the way, December 25 is also the birthday of Osiris, Adonis, and Dionysus. The newborn Krishna was presented with gold, frankincense, and myrrh. Even Christianity's weekly holy day was stolen from the pagans.[8]

"Ah," Dr. Martinez said, even before Andrea finished reading. "The Mithras myth."

"So that's a real thing, then?" Andrea asked anxiously.

"Yes," Martinez said, "if you mean the cult itself. Mithraism did exist. But was Mithras called 'Son of God' and 'Light of the World'? No. I know of no such claims in the Mithraic literature. And the Mithraic scholar Richard Gordon says unequivocally that there is 'no death, burial, and resurrection of Mithras. None.'[9]

"More to the point, however, is the question of who influenced whom. With Christianity exploding onto the scene of the Roman Empire, it is evident that other religions adopted certain teachings or practices from Christianity in order to stem the tide of departing adherents or, perhaps, to attract Christians to their side.[10]

"The key is in the dating. According to available evidences, Mithraism did not gain a foothold in the Roman Empire until after A.D. 100.[11] M. J. Vermaseran, a specialist on the cult of Mithra, certifies that no Mithraic monument can be dated earlier than the end of the first century A.D., and even the more extensive investigations at Pompeii, buried beneath the ashes of Vesuvius in A.D. 79, have not so far produced a single image of the god.[12]

She spun in her desk chair and deftly pulled a book from the shelf. "Here's a good summary by Dr. Erwin Lutzer:

> The cult of Mithras was continually evolving, adapting itself to the needs of a particular group or culture. Understandably, this religion can be interpreted in a variety of ways, and its teachings are difficult to pin down. What seems most probable is that the specific myths about Mithras' miraculous birth and becoming a 'savior god' were modeled after the stories of Jesus and developed after Christianity came to Rome in the first century."[13]

She searched the shelf on her left for another book. "It seems to me that your so-called historian in that book is guilty of what we call 'coloring the evidence.'" She flipped through the book and quickly found what she was looking for. She read: "One frequently encounters scholars who first use Christian terminology to describe pagan beliefs and practices and then marvel at the awesome parallels they think they have discovered.[14]

"Nor does similarity imply imitation. If I were born on March 28, and you were born twenty years later on the same day, it doesn't necessarily mean your parents were imitating mine."

"But some of these things seem too much to be coincidence," Matt objected.

"Oh, absolutely," Dr. Martinez admitted. "And there definitely was some integration between Christian observances and pagan customs, some of which was intentional and much of which was not. However, that goes both ways, and it's happening even today, such as when Christians of my era adapted rock songs and turned them into modern hymns. But it's ludicrous to paint such accommodation as some part of a sinister plot."

Chris nodded enthusiastically. "I agree," he said. "In fact, it made me mad when Teabing talked about Constantine changing the Christian Sabbath from Saturday to Sunday."

Martinez laughed quietly. "Would you repeat that?"

Chris answered with a smile and said, "I'll read it to you: 'Originally,' Langdon said, 'Christianity honored the Jewish Sabbath of Saturday, but Constantine shifted it to coincide with the pagan's veneration day of the sun.'"[15]

Dr. Martinez placed a palm on her chest and laughed again. "He is about two hundred fifty years late, historically speaking," Dr. Martinez offered.

"What do you mean?" Andrea asked.

Chris pulled the Bible from his hip pocket and opened it. "Long before the end of the first century, Luke recorded, 'On the first day of the week, when we were gathered together to break bread...'[16]

"In addition, Paul referred to collecting an offering on the first day of the week in 1 Corinthians 16:2.[17] And—still in the first century—the Revelation of John records that the first day of the week had come to be called 'The Lord's Day' by Christians to distinguish it from the Sabbath."[18]*

"Good grief!" Andrea said. "Langdon could have at least bothered to read the New Testament!"

Dr. Martinez nodded. "Add to the New Testament evidence the writings of the Church Fathers. Justin Martyr wrote: 'And *on the day called Sunday* there is a gathering together to one place of all those who live in cities or in the country, and the memoirs of the apostles or the writings of the prophets are read, as long as time permits.'"[19]

Did the Church suppress the sacred feminine?

"Okay," Matt said, "but even if this piece or that piece of evidence they talk about turns out to be wrong...when you put it all together, it does make you think. It's pretty persuasive."

"I don't know what you mean," Dr. Martinez said.

Matt sighed. "It's like, maybe what Teabing says about Sunday worship is wrong. Or maybe some other detail is

---

* Author's note: There are many devoted followers of Jesus who still observe the Sabbath on Saturday.

wrong. But it can't all be wrong. I mean, when he weaves together all those various strands about, you know, the pentacle and the 'sacred feminine' and those sorts of things, it gets pretty convincing."

"Are you asking me a question?" Dr. Martinez asked.

Matt frowned. "Okay. Early in the book, Langdon says that the ancient pagans, 'envisioned their world in two halves-masculine and feminine. Their gods and goddesses worked to keep a balance of power. Yin and yang.'[20] He says the original symbol for the goddesses was the pentacle, 'the representative of the *female* half of all things—a concept religious historians call the "Sacred Feminine" or the "divine goddess."'"[21]

"Yes," said Andrea. "He says the pentacle symbolizes Venus—'the goddess of female sexual love and beauty.'[22] He goes on to say that the Olympics were originally on an eight-year cycle as a tribute to her. In fact, the pentacle was almost the symbol chosen for the Olympics, and the five rings as the Olympic symbol was a last minute modification."

"He says all that?" Dr. Martinez asked, a smile teasing the corners of her mouth.

"Uh huh," Andrea said. "He says that the early Jews also believed in a male *and* a female deity. Here it is:

> Early Jews believed that the Holy of Holies in Solomon's Temple housed not only God but also his powerful female equal, Shekinah. ...The Jewish tetragrammaton YHWH—the sacred name of God—in fact derived from Jehovah, an androgynous physical union between the masculine *Jah* and the pre-Hebraic name for Eve—*Havah*."[23]

Dr. Martinez and Chris both opened their mouths to speak, but Andrea didn't give them the opportunity. "And this becomes important to the whole story," she said, "because later in the book we learn how the church changed all that and basically wiped out the sacred feminine from Christianity."

By the time Andrea finished, Dr. Martinez blinked and stared as if in shock. "Oh, my," she said, eventually. She picked up a pen from her desk and began making notes.

"All right," she said at last. "First, although I am no expert on the pentacle, we know from authoritative sources that there exists no single interpretation of the pentacle and its origins. Even within Wicca, the neo-pagan religion to which the pentacle is central, there is no agreed-upon, universal meaning. Kerr Cuhulian, a spokesman for Wicca, has said, 'There seems to have been no single tradition concerning their meaning and use, and in many contexts they seem simply to have been decorative.'[24] And another Wiccan, Doreen Valiente says, 'The origin of the magical five-pointed star is lost in the mists of time.[25] Pythagoras [B.C. 570-495], the Greek mathematician, interpreted it to mean 'health.'[26] Empedocles [B.C. 490-430] used it to symbolize spirit, earth, air, fire, and water.[27] Even modern neopagans use it to represent spirituality over materialism.[28] But I know of *no* scholarly sources that interpret the pentacle as representing the sacred feminine.

"As for the Olympics," she continued, "the historical sources I am familiar with make it clear that the Olympic Games were a tribute to Zeus, not Venus.[29] This fact is so indisputable that I should be embarrassed for any historian who asserts otherwise...with a straight face, that is."

She consulted the notes she had scrawled and turned to pull a book from the shelf behind her. "As for the claim that the Olympic rings are related to the pentacle, I find that totally mystifying. The rings are a modern symbol, designed by Baron Pierre de Coubertin in 1913 and adopted in 1920." She opened the book and placed it where Matt, Andrea, and Chris could all see the page. "It was intended to represent the five continents, considering North and South America as one.[30]

"Oh, and as for the ancient Jews worshiping goddesses—while there was a recurring problem in Jewish history with temple prostitution and the worship of certain female deities, this was clearly against the Law of Moses, the prophets, and Jewish tradition.[31] Jewish theology and tradition unequivocally supported the worship of and allegiance to one God, Yahweh.

"And that idea about Shekinah being a female equivalent of Yahweh, why, that's just laughable."

Chris pulled a single leaf from his copy of *The Da Vinci Code.* "I have a quote from Professor Darrell Bock, Research Professor of New Testament Studies at Dallas Theological Seminary." Martinez nodded as though she knew what Chris was about to read. "He defines *Shekinah* as 'a term referring to the "glory of God." The idea that this term is paired with the name of God, Yahweh, so that a male (Yahweh) and female (Shekinah) counterpart exists with God, is simple fabrication."[32]

"Likewise fabricated," Dr. Martinez said, "is the statement that Yahweh came from the word Jehovah. This is exactly backwards. You see, ancient written Hebrew had no vowels. So the 'original' covenant name of God was written with four letters: yod, hey, vav, and hey. But Jewish scribes, inserting the vowels from 'adonai,' the Hebrew word for 'Lord,' between those four letters produced a pronounceable name for God: Yahowah. When that word was Latinized, around A.D. 1270, the *Y* changed to a *J* and the *W* to a *V*. Thus, the name Jehovah entered into usage...but in exactly the opposite order as what you read to me.[33]

"And just one more thing," Dr. Martinez said as though she were imposing on their schedules instead of the other way around. "The statement that the name Jehovah was supposedly a union between the masculine *Jah* and the 'pre-Hebraic' name for Eve—*Havah*—suggests to me that someone is making a joke."[34]

"A joke?" Matt asked.

"*Havah* was, in fact, the actual *Hebrew* name given to Adam's wife; there's nothing 'pre-Hebraic' about it.[35] The word means 'life,' by the way, because she was called 'the mother of all the living.'[36] But, think about it: if the original

43

Old Testament documents were written in Hebrew, what pre-Hebraic documents could the expert in your book possibly have consulted in order to gain the information he seems to know?"

Matt shrugged helplessly. "I don't know."

"Of course not," Dr. Martinez answered. "No one could."

Was the early church anti-feminine?

"So the whole thing's just a crock?" Matt stood. "So if *everything* in this book is so totally wrong, then how can it sell so many copies? How come it's been made into a movie? How can so many people believe it?"

Andrea looked at Matt, her eyes wide.

"How am I supposed to know," he continued, "who the liars are here? How can I know whether Teabing is full of it...or *you* are?"

Dr. Martinez didn't seem offended by Matt's outburst. "Some people can't until they conduct their own investigation...compare sources...weigh the evidence. Others, at least in my experience, just seem to have an ear for the truth." She looked at Andrea.

Andrea blushed. "They say in the book," she said, hesitatingly, "that Constantine and the Church purposely arranged the Bible to get rid of the sacred feminine and put men in charge. I'd like to know if that part is true. Even some of it."

Dr. Martinez glanced at Matt as though silently asking if he planned to leave or stay. He finally returned to his chair, the muscles in his jaw tight.

Andrea turned to read from her book. "It says that 'Constantine and his male successors successfully converted the world from matriarchal paganism to patriarchal Christianity.'[37] It says, 'powerful men in the early Christian church "conned" the world by propagating lies that devalued the female and tipped the scales in favor of the masculine.'"[38]

Before responding, Martinez turned and plucked yet another book from the shelf to her left. She opened it and then calmly offered it to Matt. "Matt," she said, her tone kind, "would you be so kind as to read—this paragraph?" She indicated a passage with her finger.

Matt straightened and took the book. He read: "Ancient paganism was neither matriarchal nor patriarchal. It was not even close to a unified belief system....Instead of there being any single 'matriarchal paganism,' there actually existed *many different paganisms*. Some did not even involve a goddess.[39]

"Okay," Matt said, as he returned the book to Dr. Martinez. "But I think he still has a point when he points out that there are today no female Orthodox rabbis, Catholic priests, or Islamic clerics.[40] So whatever they did must have worked."

"Are you saying that, according to this book, Constantine and the fourth century church were so successful at suppressing the 'sacred feminine' as to affect Orthodox Judaism, which is centuries older than Christianity, *and* Islam, which wouldn't even be born for another three hundred years? That's an extraordinary claim!

"More to the point, however, it must be emphasized that neither the Scriptures nor the early Christians were anti-female—far from it. For example, the Bible does not blame Eve for original sin, and it's ludicrous, by the way, to imply that the doctrine of original sin originated during the middle ages or even after the time of Constantine when the Genesis account is much, much older than both. On the contrary, Romans 5:12 says that through one *man* sin entered the world, naming that man as Adam and labeling that sin as 'the offense of Adam.'[41]

"In addition, if the Bible—as it's been known since before the days of Constantine—were anti-female, there would be no accounts of Deborah's leadership, Jael's courage, Ruth's loyalty, Abigail's diplomacy, Esther's heroism, or Phoebe's service. If the Bible were anti-female, we would never have heard of Philip's prophesying daughters, Aquila's wife Priscilla, or Paul's coworker Junia.

"If the Bible—as we have it today—were anti-female, we would surely not know that Jesus' band of disciples did include women—Mary Magdalene among them. One of the first 'evangelists' recorded in Scripture was a woman, who ran into her Samaritan village and spread the news to the entire community.[42] Jesus' first post-resurrection appearance was to Mary Magdalene, and the gospel writers honor her as not only the first person to see the resurrected Christ, but also the first person commissioned to spread the good news.[43]

"And in the earliest decades of church life, Paul the Apostle, though raised and educated in a thoroughly patriarchal tradition, nonetheless, enunciated a universal principle to the church: 'There is neither Jew nor Greek, there is neither slave nor free man, there is neither male nor female; for you are all one in Christ Jesus.'[44] In what was probably his earliest letter, written about A.D. 49, he exalted the female as equally 'sacred' to the male on the basis of Christian unity in Jesus Christ, a revolutionary statement for that day and age."

What effect did Constantine have on church history?

"Wow," said Andrea. "I never knew that."

"But," Matt interjected, "that doesn't necessarily mean Constantine didn't try to undermine the sacred feminine. And the main point that Constantine basically hijacked Jesus from his original followers and made him divine in order to expand their own power—still seems believable." [45]

Dr. Martinez smiled broadly again. She pointed to Matt's copy of *The Da Vinci Code*. "Can you show me where it says that?"

Matt began leafing through the book. "It's all through it, really, but...." He finally stopped, scanned a page, and then handed the book to Dr. Martinez. She read:

"I thought Constantine was a Christian," Sophie said.

"Hardly," Teabing scoffed. "He was a lifelong pagan who was baptized on his deathbed, too weak to protest...."[46]

She scanned down a few paragraphs, seeing statements and topics they'd already discussed.

Sophie was surprised. "Why would a pagan emperor choose *Christianity* as the official religion?"

Teabing chuckled. "Constantine was a very good businessman. He could see that Christianity was on the rise, and he simply backed the winning horse. Historians still marvel at the brilliance with which Constantine converted the sun-worshipping pagans to Christianity. By fusing pagan symbols, dates, and rituals into the growing Christian tradition, he created a kind of hybrid religion that was acceptable to both parties."[47]

Dr. Martinez lifted her gaze from the book and shook her head wonderingly. "I—I'm speechless," she said. "I wouldn't accept work like this from my undergrads." She resumed reading, eventually settling on the following:

"During this fusion of religions, Constantine needed to strengthen the new Christian tradition, and held a famous ecumenical gathering known as the Council of Nicaea."

Sophie had heard of it only insofar as its being the birthplace of the Nicene Creed.

"At this gathering," Teabing said, "many aspects of Christianity were debated and voted upon—the date of Easter, the role of the bishops, the administration of sacraments, and, of course, the *divinity* of Jesus."

47

"I don't follow. His divinity?"

"My dear," Teabing declared, "until *that* moment in history, Jesus was viewed by His followers as a mortal prophet . . . a great and powerful man, but a *man* nonetheless. A mortal."

"Not the Son of God?"

"Right," Teabing said. "Jesus' establishment as 'the Son of God' was officially proposed and voted on by the Council of Nicaea."

"Hold on. You're saying Jesus' divinity was the result of a *vote?*"

"A relatively close vote at that," Teabing added....[48]

Martinez closed the book, set it on her desk, closed her eyes, and pinched the bridge of her nose with her thumb and forefinger. Finally, she swallowed and looked up, and it became clear that she had been struggling to suppress laughter. "I'm sorry," she said. "This is very unprofessional." She inhaled deeply and finally managed to gather her composure.

"All right," she said. "Let's talk about the facts." She reached for one of the books she had pulled off the shelf earlier and set on her desk. She opened it and extended it—this time—to Andrea, pointing to a spot on page three. "Would you read these three paragraphs?"

Andrea took the book and read aloud:

Church historians agree that next to the events in the New Testament, the most important event in the history of Christianity is the conversion of Emperor Constantine to Christianity in A.D. 312. In brief, here's the story: Constantine's troops were positioned at the Milvian Bridge just outside of

Rome, where they were preparing to overthrow the Roman emperor Maxentius. A victory would, in effect, make Constantine the sole ruler of the empire. But the night before the battle, Constantine saw a vision that changed his life and the history of the church.

"In the words of Eusebius of Caesarea, who was both a historian and a confidant of Constantine, the emperor was praying to a pagan god when 'he saw with his own eyes the trophy of a cross in the light of the heavens, above the sun and an inscription, *Conquer By This*, attached to it.... Then in his sleep the Christ of God appeared to him with the sign which he had seen in the heavens, and commanded him to make a likeness of the sign which he had seen in the heavens, and to use it as a safeguard in all engagements with this enemies.'[49]

"To make a long story short, Constantine crossed over the bridge and won the battle, fighting under the banner of the Christian cross. Later he issued the Edict of Milan, decreeing that Christians were no longer to be persecuted."[50]

Martinez thanked Andrea and reclaimed the book from her. "Generally speaking, credible historians do not doubt the sincerity of Constantine's conversion, but they do recognize that one did not become—or remain—emperor without a great deal of ambition and maneuvering."

She sprang from her chair and strode around her desk to the corner of the bookshelves nearest the door. She pulled yet another volume from the shelf and returned to her seat. "Paul L. Maier, Professor of Ancient History at Western Michigan University, summarizes what almost all historians believe about Constantine: 'While Constantine was undeniably a flawed individual, historians agree that he certainly abjured paganism, [and] became a genuine Christian convert.'"[51]

She shut the book. "I think the worst thing about Constantine's position toward the church is that he brought political values into a church that had been purified by persecution. Making Christianity an acceptable religion in the Roman Empire was probably one of the worst things that could have happened to the church as multitudes of professing Christians were encouraged to join the church who, in reality, did not trust Christ alone for salvation and continued to practice their old religions, bringing some of those practices into the church. Some would say—and I would agree—that persecution tends to purge the worst and bring out the best in the church."

She paused for a moment as though her last statement had reminded her of something. "But, to be fair, that was not Constantine's problem. His problem, like all emperors, was preserving the unity of the empire.

"So, when a forceful speaker named Arius began to attract and mobilize a large following of people who were persuaded that Christ was something less than eternal God, something like a lesser God, Constantine felt both a political and religious desire to end the controversy. So he called together over three hundred bishops from all over the empire." She traded the book in her hands for the book she had reclaimed from Andrea and opened it to read:

> [Constantine] gave the opening speech himself, telling the delegates that doctrinal disunity was worse than war.

> This intrusion of a politician into the doctrines and procedures of the church was resented by some of the delegates, but welcomed by others. For those who had gone through a period of bitter persecution, this conference, carried on under the imperial banner, was heaven on earth.[52]

"So, it is true, then," said Matt. "Constantine did arrange a vote on the divinity of Jesus."

What was the Council of Nicaea?

"Constantine did call the council," Martinez corrected. "And the bishops debated the precise meaning of *what had been written in the Scriptures centuries before.*

"But by no means should you understand that Jesus' establishment as 'the Son of God' was officially proposed and voted on by the Council of Nicaea as that book said." Her eyes blazed with intensity, and her slight accent was suddenly not so slight. "That is an ignorant statement. However, do not take my word for it. Listen to Peter's words as recorded in Matthew's gospel, written more than two hundred years before the Council of Nicaea. In what is called 'The Great Confession,' Peter told Jesus, "You are the Christ, the Son of the living God."[53]

"Mark's gospel, likewise written more than two hundred years before the Council of Nicaea, reports the words of the Roman centurion on Jesus' crucifixion detail: 'Truly this man was the Son of God!'[54]

"Luke's gospel—do I need to say it?—written more than two hundred years before the Council of Nicaea, relates accounts of demons, that Jesus had cast out of people, as shouting, 'You are the Son of God!'[55]

"And John, the 'beloved disciple,' wrote of Jesus, when he began his gospel—*also* written more than two hundred years before the Council of Nicaea:

> In the beginning was the Word, and the Word was with God, and the Word was God. He was in the beginning with God. All things came into being through Him, and apart from Him nothing came into being.... And the Word became flesh, and dwelt among us, and we saw His glory, glory as of the only begotten from the Father, full of grace and truth.[56]

"To put forward that 'Jesus' establishment as "the Son of God" was officially proposed and voted on by the Council of Nicaea' does not bring shame on Jesus, nor on his followers, but on any serious historian who would propose such a thing in the face of all evidence to the contrary! I am just scratching the surface in what I have said so far, but these followers of Christ clearly regarded Jesus as the Son of God.

"And not only those first disciples," she continued, "but also some of the most influential and outspoken first and second-century followers of Christ had the same belief. Justin Martyr wrote of Christ, 'being the first-begotten Word of God, is even God'; 'both God and Lord of hosts.'[57] Irenaeus referred to Jesus as 'our Lord, and God, and Saviour, and King.'[58] Clement of Alexandria called him 'truly most manifest Deity, He that is made equal to the Lord of the universe; because he was His Son.'"[59]

Shuffling books again, she picked up one of the volumes on her desk and flipped a few pages. "Professor Maier states, 'The Council of Nicaea did not debate over whether Jesus was divine or only mortal, but whether he was coeternal with the Father.'"[60]

Andrea shifted in her chair. "But," she said, referring to *The Da Vinci Code*, "the book says that Constantine and the Council of Nicaea threw out all the stuff that showed Jesus was only a man and put in all that other stuff."

"I will say two things in answer to that," Dr. Martinez said. "The first is this: There is no historical evidence that the Council of Nicaea discussed the Gnostic gospels or anything pertaining to the canon. You will not find a single line in historical accounts or studies relating to Nicaea that even hints about a debate concerning what books to include in the New Testament. Dr. Lutzer points out, 'Twenty rulings were issued at Nicaea, and the contents of all of them are still in existence; not one of them refers to issues regarding the canon.'[61]

"The second thing I will say is this," she continued, leaning back and striking a more philosophical tone. "If

Constantine included only those gospels that supported Jesus' divinity, then how is it that the early and authentic Gospels included in the Bible to this day speak clearly of Jesus' human traits? They speak of his physical, mental, and social development. They speak of his hunger, his amazement, his anger, his fatigue, and his sorrow.[62] In the book of Hebrews, we are told that not only did Christ suffer temptation but that he can completely understand when we are tempted because he was 'in all points tempted *like as we are.*'[63] The Bible very clearly paints a picture of Jesus as fully human *and* fully divine."

Chris nodded slowly as Dr. Martinez paused, and Andrea and Matt seemed to ponder her words.

But Martinez was not finished. "May I ask *you* a question?"

"Me?" Matt asked, poking his chest with his thumb.

"All three of you," she answered.

They shrugged, almost in unison. "Sure," Andrea answered.

"If it is true, as your fictional character suggests, that until *that* moment in history, Jesus was viewed by his followers as a mere mortal...where did Constantine get the gospels that said otherwise?"

Andrea's eyes widened. "Oh, I see what you mean," she said.

"Nice try," Matt said. "But the book said there were over eighty gospels to choose from. Obviously some emphasized the humanity of Jesus and other documents emphasized his divinity."

"But your fictional character did not say that up until the fourth century A.D. there was some *confusion* among the followers of Jesus or *competition* among various sects about the relationship between Jesus' humanity and divinity; he said—I think I can nearly quote it—that until *that* moment in history, Jesus was viewed by his followers as a mortal. Period. End of story. Is that not what he said?"

Andrea turned to Matt and spoke animatedly. "She's right, Matt. That's exactly what Teabing said."

"Whatever," Matt said, waving a hand.

Andrea turned to Dr. Martinez. "I see what you mean. It would have to be one or the other. If there were some gospels that Constantine chose to emphasize Jesus' divinity, destroying the others, then the idea of Jesus as the Son of God couldn't have been a new concept introduced for purely political purposes. He totally contradicts himself."

Dr. Martinez nodded slowly.

"But something still bothers me," Andrea admitted.

"What is that?" Dr. Martinez asked.

"It's that part about the vote. It seems like, if the Council of Nicaea voted and just barely agreed that Jesus was both human and divine, then maybe it could just as easily have gone the other way. You know? Maybe if someone hadn't been sick that day or something like that, the whole thing would have turned out different."

"Thank you for asking that question," Dr. Martinez said. "I might have forgotten that point." She picked up *The Da Vinci Code* from her desk where it had reposed all this time and found the pages she had read earlier. "Yes, here it is. This Teabing character says the divinity of Jesus was established by 'a relatively close vote at that.'"[64] She lifted her gaze to Andrea and smiled. "Would you like to know exactly how close?"

Andrea nodded.

Martinez spoke slowly. "Three hundred...to two."[65]

"Three hundred—?"

"To two," Martinez repeated. "That's quite a stretch to call that 'a relatively close vote,' isn't it?"

"Sure is," Andrea agreed.

"In short," Dr. Martinez concluded, "when all was said and done, 99.33 percent of the church leadership throughout the entire Roman Empire endorsed what has come to be called the Nicene Creed, which is recited in many churches to this day. It says:

We believe in one God the Father Almighty,
Maker of heaven and earth, and of all things visible and invisible.

'And in one Lord Jesus Christ, the only-begotten Son of God,
begotten of the Father before all worlds,
God of God, Light of Light, Very God of Very God,
begotten, not made, being of one substance with the Father
by whom all things were made;
who for us men and for our salvation
came down from heaven,
and was incarnate by the Holy Ghost
of the Virgin Mary,
and was made man;
and was crucified also for us under Pontius Pilate;
he suffered and was buried;
and the third day he rose again
according to the Scriptures,
and ascended into heaven,
and sitteth on the right hand of the Father;
and he shall come again, with glory,
to judge both the quick and the dead;
whose kingdom shall have no end.

'And we believe in the Holy Ghost,
the Lord and Giver of Life,
who proceedeth from the Father and the Son;
who with the Father and the Son together
is worshipped and glorified;
who spake by the prophets.

'And we believe in one holy catholic and apostolic Church;
we acknowledge one baptism for the remission of sins;
and we look for the resurrection of the dead,
and the life of the world to come. AMEN.'[66]

An awed silence filled the room when Dr. Martinez finished her recitation of the seventeen-hundred-year-old phrases. A few moments later, Chris, Matt, and Andrea left, the creed having become their benediction.

55

Chapter Three Notes

1. 232.
2. Acts 17:22-23.
3. Richard Abanes, *The Truth Behind the Da Vinci Code* (Eugene, OR: Harvest House Publishers, 2004), 33.
4. 232.
5. Erwin W. Lutzer, *The Da Vinci Deception* (Wheaton, IL: Tyndale House Publishers, 2004), 3, 4.
6. 232.
7. Matthew 4:43-44, 46-47; John 18:36, NASB.
8. 232.
9. Richard Gordon, *Image and Value in the Greco-Roman World* (Aldershot, UK: Variorum, 1996), 96.
10. Bruce M. Metzger, "Mystery Religions and Early Christianity," in *Historical and Literary Studies* (Leiden, Netherlands: E.J. Brill, 1968), 11.
11. Edwin M. Yamauchi, *Pre-Christian Gnosticism,* 2nd ed. (Grand Rapids, MI: Baker Book House, 1983), 112.
12. M.J. Vermaseran, *Mithras: The Secret God* (London: Chatto and Windus, 1963).
13. Lutzer, *Da Vinci Deception,* 96-97.
14. Ronald Nash, *Christianity and the Hellenistic World* (Grand Rapids, MI: Zondervan Publishing House, 1984), 126.
15. 232-233.
16. Acts 20:7, NASB.
17. "On the first day of every week each one of you is to put aside and save, as he may prosper, so that no collections be made when I come."
18. Revelation 1:10.
19. *First Apology,* in *The Ante-Nicene Fathers,* vol. 1, eds. James Donaldson and Alexander Roberts (Grand Rapids, MI: Eerdmans, 1993), 1.67.
20. 36.
21. Ibid.
22. Ibid.
23. 309.
24. Kerr Cuhulian, *Full Contact Magick: A Book of Shadows for the Wiccan Warrior* (St. Paul, MN: Llewellyn Publications, 2002), 239.
25. Dorreen Valiente, *An ABC of Witchcraft Past & Present* (New York: St. Martin's Press, 1973), 306.
26. John Michael Greer, *The New Encyclopedia of the Occult* (St. Paul, MN: Llewellyn Publications, 2003), 367.
27. Raven Grimassi, *Encyclopedia of Wicca & Witchcraft* (St. Paul, MN: Llewellyn Publications, 2000), 285.
28. Cuhulian, *Full Contact Magick,* 103.

29. M.I. Finley and H.W. Pieket, *The Olympic Games: The First Thousand Years* (New York: Viking, 1976); A. Dailey and J. Kieran, *The Story of the Olympic Games* (Philadelphia: Lippincott, 1977); B. Henry and R. Yeoman, *An Approved History of the Olympic Games* (Sherman Oaks, CA: Alfred, 1984); and Allen Guttman, *The Olympics: A History of the Modern Games* (Urbana, IL: University of Illinois Press, 1992).

30. "Torch Run, Olympic Rings Not So Ancient." *The Herald-Mail,* July 14, 1996, accessed at www.Herald-mail.com/news/1996/olympics/july14herald.html.

31. Deuteronomy 23:17-18; 1 Kings 11:33.

32. Darrell Bock, *Breaking the Da Vinci Code* (Nashville: Thomas Nelson Publishers, 2004), 187.

33. Richard Abanes, *The Truth Behind the Da Vinci Code,* 19.

34. 309.

35. David H. Stern's, *The Complete Jewish Bible* (Clarksville, MD: Jewish New Testament Press, 1998), 4.

36. Genesis 3:20.

37. 124.

38. Ibid.

39. Abanes, *The Truth Behind the Da Vinci Code*, 33.

40. 125.

41. Romans 5:14, NASB.

42. John 4:28-30.

43. John 20:17-18.

44. Galatians 3:28.

45. 233.

46. 232.

47. Ibid.

48. 233.

49. Mark A. Noll, *Turning Points: Decisive Moments in the History of Christianity* (Grand Rapids, MI: Baker Book House, 1997), 50.

50. Lutzer, *Da Vinci Deception*, 3, 4.

51. Hanegraaff and Maier, *Da Vinci Fact or Fiction*, 14.

52. Lutzer, *Da Vinci Deception*, 5.

53. Matthew 16:16, NASB.

54. Mark 15:39, NASB.

55. Luke 4:41, NASB.

56. John 1:1-3, 14, NASB.

57. *First Apology* in *The Ante-Nicene Fathers, vol.1,* 184.

58. Irenaeus, *Against Heresies,* in *The Ante-Nicene Fathers,* vol. 1, 330.

59. Clement of Alexandria, "Exhortation to the Heathen," in *The Ante-Nicene Fathers,* 202.

60. Hanegraaff and Maier, *Da Vinci Fact or Fiction*, 15.

61. Lutzer, *Da Vinci Deception*, 14-15. Lutzer also seems to have tracked down the source of the erroneous view of those who

believe the canon was an issue at the Nicene Council. A Baron D'Holbach in *Ecce Homo* affirmed that the belief was fiction spread by the famous French atheist, Voltaire (1694-1778). The original source for Voltaire, however, turns out to be an "anonymous document called *Vetus Synodicon*, written in about A.D. 887" which "devotes a chapter to each of the ecumenical councils held until that time." Lutzer continues, "...the compiler adds details not found in the writings of historians. As for his account of Nicaea, he writes that the council dealt with matters of the divinity of Jesus, the Trinity, and the canon. He writes, 'The canonical and apocryphal books it distinguished in the following manner: in the house of God the books were placed down by the holy altar; then the council asked the Lord in prayer that the inspired words be found on top and—as in fact happened...' That, quite obviously, is the stuff of legend. No primary documents pertaining to Nicaea make reference to such a procedure" (16).

62. Luke 2:52; Matthew 4:2, 8:5-10; Mark 11:15-17; Luke 8:22-23; and John 11:33-36, respectively.
63. Hebrews 4:15-16, KJV.
64. 233.
65. See Hanegraaff and Maier, *Da Vinci Fact or Fiction*, 15; and Lutzer, *Da Vinci Deception*, 8, among others.
66. The word "catholic" in the creed doesn't mean only the Roman Catholic Church; it means "universal," and so it refers to the single true church around the world, which includes people of every nation, color, class, race, and background.

Chapter Four
"What Does That Tell You?"

Chris saw Matt waiting for him outside The Daily Grind. He clapped his friend on the shoulder and greeted him with, "Where's Andrea?"

Matt shrugged. "I don't know. She never called last night, so I kind of figured she was either out with friends or up late studying."

They entered the coffee shop, and instead of their usual spot, they chose a table in a corner. Both men set down several books before ordering their drinks. The three friends had agreed to do some research on their own before they met again. Chris suggested avenues to explore, and this was their first get-together since then.

"So," Chris began when he and Matt settled into their chairs, "how did your research go?"

Matt scrunched his nose. "All right, I guess. I didn't get as far as I wanted to. I think I just scratched the surface." Matt's assignment had been to research *The Da Vinci Code*'s fascinating claims about Leonardo da Vinci and his work. "I haven't even had time to organize my research very well."

Chris sipped his drink, smacking his lips afterward. "Tell me what you found," he said.

Matt spread out a few note-filled sheets of notebook paper on the table surface. "I have to keep reminding myself," Matt said, "it's just a novel. But still, it's frustrating to try to sort through what's accurate and what's not."

"For example?" Chris prodded.

Are all descriptions of artwork, architecture, etc., accurate?

"Okay. The book says that 'all descriptions of artwork, architecture, documents, and secret rituals in this novel are accurate,' right?"[1]

Chris nodded.

"So, one of the first things I did was check out the Louvre Museum, through its official website."[2]

"Great idea," Chris acknowledged.

"But right there—as I was just getting started—I found an inaccuracy in *The Da Vinci Code*." He opened his copy. "The book says that at President Mitterrand's explicit demand, the famous glass pyramid had been constructed of exactly six hundred sixty-six panes of glass."[3]

Chris nodded. "Yeah...so?"

"The number is six hundred seventy-three."[4]

"No kidding."

It was Matt's turn to nod. "Now, on the one hand, I can understand playing with the facts there because he goes on to say the six hundred sixty-six number had become 'a hot topic among conspiracy buffs who claimed 666 was the number of Satan.'"[5]

"Yeah," Chris agreed. "It's just a novel."

"Except it still bugs me because he said all descriptions of architecture in the book are accurate."

Andrea suddenly appeared beside them, hefting a satchel of books onto the table. "Sorry I'm late," she said, breathless.

"Where have you been?" Matt asked.

She rolled her eyes. "You're not going to believe this. I didn't sleep last night."

"Why? What's wrong?" Matt said.

"Nothing's wrong, I just stayed up all night doing this." She started pulling out a series of books and stacked them on the table. She and Chris chatted for a few minutes while Matt went to the counter to order Andrea's Chai tea. When he returned, Chris filled Matt in.

"I was just telling her what you'd been saying about the panes of glass in the pyramid."

"I'd just gotten started," Matt said. He sat down. "Mostly, the descriptions of artwork in the book seem pretty accurate. But not totally.

60

"There seemed to be a little more substance to Langdon's contention in the book that the Mona Lisa was painted by Leonardo as a self-portrait. There is some uncertainty among scholars about who the image depicts. Some recent researchers have used 'morphing' techniques to try to show that the portrait bears a striking resemblance to Leonardo.[6] But then, all contemporary documents refer to the sitter for the portrait as a woman, and—contrary to popular opinion—there are no definitive portraits of Leonardo.[7] Most art experts believe the real-life Mona Lisa was Lisa Gherardini or, less probably, Isabella of Aragon. But then Langdon goes on to say that the title *Mona Lisa* refers to the Egyptian gods Amon and Isis."[8]

"Ooh, I know," Andrea said. "I thought that part was fascinating."

Matt frowned. "Except Leonardo never came up with name 'Mona Lisa.' It was never even used in his lifetime."

"How's that possible?" Andrea asked. "He painted it, didn't he?"

"Yes, but the name 'Mona Lisa' wasn't used until the nineteenth century. 'Mona' is short for 'madonna,' meaning simply 'lady,' and Lisa is just the name of the most likely subject of the painting. In Italian and among scholars, it's more commonly known as 'La Gioconda,' which refers to Lisa Gherardini's married name. So that whole thing about 'Amon L'Isa' is a total fraud because Leonardo never called it 'Mona Lisa.'[9]

"The depiction of Leonardo's *Madonna of the Rocks*—oh, and by the way, here's something I never knew: apparently art scholars do not call him 'Da Vinci,' the way the book's characters do because that's just a reference to where he was born. From everything I've read, Leonardo is always 'Leonardo' among artsy people.

"But I couldn't find any evidence at all for the claim that Leonardo 'horrified' church officials by filling the painting with 'explosive and disturbing details.'[10] And the book describes the angel Uriel as 'making a cutting gesture as if slicing the invisible head gripped by Mary's claw-like hand.'"[11] He produced a color photocopy of the painting and showed it to Andrea and Chris. "Is that what you see?"

Andrea and Chris studied the painting for a moment until Andrea answered, "It just looks like he's pointing."

"Exactly. But the worst part is this. Remember the scene where Sophie basically backs down the museum guard by threatening to rip the *Madonna of the Rocks?*"

Chris and Andrea nodded.

"Here's what Bruce Boucher, the curator of European decorative arts and sculpture at the Art Institute of Chicago, wrote in *The New York Times*:

> It is also breathtaking to read that the heroine, Sophie Neveu, uses one of Leonardo's paintings, 'The Madonna of the Rocks,' as a shield, pressing it so close to her body that it bends. More than six feet tall and painted on wood, not canvas, the 'Madonna' is unlikely to be so supple.[12]

"Yet, the book clearly claims, it was 'a five-foot-tall canvas.' It's not canvas, and my research shows that it's actually *six-and-a-half* feet tall. So much for 'All descriptions of artwork' being accurate.'"[13]

"That's good research on your part, though," Chris said.

"But it's still disappointing."

"Why?" Andrea said, a teasing tone in her voice. "It's fiction, right?"

Matt shot her a look. "More and more," he said.

Was Mary Magdalene pictured in The Last Supper?

"But what about *The Last Supper*?" Andrea asked. "That's the one I really want to know about."

He nodded. "I did get some information, but there's a lot I still want to check into." Matt fished out a color photocopy and placed it on the table. "Okay. We all know that Teabing makes a big deal out of showing that Mary Magdelene is depicted sitting next to Jesus in Leonardo's famous painting, right?" He poked the page, pointing out the figure seated to the right of Jesus in the image.

"First, he makes the point that there is not one cup in the painting but actually thirteen cups, which is supposed to be our first hint that the Holy Grail is not a cup but a person. The book says:

> Teabing was grinning smugly. Sophie looked down at the painting, seeing to her astonishment that everyone at the table had a glass of wine, including Christ. Thirteen cups. Moreover, the cups were tiny, stemless, and made of glass. There was no chalice in the painting. No Holy Grail." [14]

"Can I say something?" Chris asked.

Matt nodded.

"I didn't catch this the first time I read the book because all this talk about *The Last Supper* was fascinating, but this time, it dawned on me: Teabing treats *The Last Supper* as if it were a photo of the actual event...as though Leonardo had been there and knew every detail of the historical event itself...instead of what it is: an artistic interpretation painted more than a thousand years later!" He turned pages in his copy of *The Da Vinci Code*. "And listen to what Teabing says next. This really gets me. It says:

> Teabing's eyes twinkled. 'A bit strange, don't you think, considering that both the Bible and our standard Grail legend celebrate this moment as the definitive arrival of the Holy Grail. Oddly, Da Vinci appears to have forgotten to paint the Cup of Christ.' [15]

"That's just absurd!" Chris continued. "The Bible says no such thing. [16] In fact, the gospel accounts refer only to Jesus using a cup. No Bible scholar or informed historian would be surprised at all that there is no fancy jewel-encrusted chalice in Leonardo's painting; that's the stuff of legend, not history!"

"I didn't know that," Matt said, nodding. "But let's talk about the person next to Jesus now, who Teabing says is Mary Magdalene. He points out 'flowing red hair, delicate folded hands, and the hint of a bosom.'"[17]

"Do you see the hint of a bosom?" Chris asked Andrea.

She leaned close to the photocopy and studied it. Finally, she shook her head. "I think this guy—" she said, pointing to the bearded figure on Jesus' left— "has more of a bosom than that one!"

Chris chuckled softly. "I see what you mean."

Matt continued. "He also makes his case based on Jesus and the figure to his right being 'clothed as mirror images of one another,' forming an indisputable V-shape—representing the female womb—by the way they were sitting, and 'the unquestionable outline of an enormous, flawlessly formed letter M' formed by the shapes of Jesus and the person at his right, perhaps representing *Matrimonio* or *Mary Magdalene*."[18]

"Do you see that?" Chris asked Andrea.

She frowned. "I see a 'V,'" she admitted, "but I can't see how anyone would think this represents an 'M.'" She traced the forms of the figures on the photocopy.

Matt nodded. "So, let me tell you what I've discovered. About halfway through my research it dawned on me that even if Leonardo was trying to tell us that Mary Magdalene was the Holy Grail, his belief doesn't mean it's true. I mean, Leonardo lived almost fifteen centuries after Jesus, right?[19] He wasn't exactly a firsthand observer if you know what I mean."

Andrea agreed quickly. "Yeah, that makes sense. But do you think it's Mary? Instead of John, I mean."

"I found a *Slate* magazine article that I thought put it well. It said:

Look closely at the figure to Jesus' right, Brown says; it's obviously a woman. What any art historian could tell him is that the figure, always thought to be St. John the Apostle, resembles other Leonardo portraits of biblical figures as effeminate men. If Da Vinci thought John looked like a girly man, that's one thing. But a girlish-looking figure in a painting isn't proof that Mary was present at the Last Supper, let alone that Jesus and Mary were married. (And, by the way, if Mary was sitting in John's seat at the Last Supper, where was John?)[20]

"And everything I've researched so far says that in Leonardo's day John was also shown as young and beardless. Bruce Boucher, the scholar I quoted earlier, said this is the way Florentine artists traditionally depicted John.[21] Even more specifically, portrayals of the Last Supper by other artists of the period also show a beardless John sitting right next to Jesus."

"That makes sense," Chris said, "since the Bible account of the Last Supper depicts John sitting close enough to Jesus to lay his head on Jesus' chest."[22]

"Okay, but what about the clothes?" Andrea asked. "I mean, all that stuff about the letter *V* and the letter *M* seems kind of lame to me, but he does have a point about their clothes being like mirror images of each other."

"I haven't gotten that far in my research," Matt admitted.

"I wouldn't be surprised to find out that that has more to do with art than theology," Chris said. "After all, as a master artist, Leonardo may have chosen colors and shades and shapes for their compositional value, don't you think?"

"Of course," Matt said.

"Look at this, too," Andrea said. "See this guy?" She pointed to a man on Jesus' right. "And this one?" She pointed to a figure on the opposite side. "One is wearing green with an orangeish wrap, and the other is just the opposite."

"So maybe those two guys were married, too," Chris joked. He turned his gaze on Matt. "What about Peter's supposedly menacing look? And the dagger in his hand, implying that Peter was jealous of Mary?[23] Did you find out anything about that?"

"A little bit," Matt said. "For starters, I think it just looks like he is leaning in to talk to the figure next to Jesus, which matches up with the scholarship. I haven't yet found a single scholarly source that doesn't agree with the conventional opinion that Leonardo painted this scene to depict the disciples' reactions after Jesus said that one of them betray him."

"If that's the case," Chris said, "then Leonardo knew his New Testament...because one of the Gospels says that after Jesus made that startling announcement Peter told John to ask Jesus who he meant."[24]

"And at least one scholar says the hand holding a dagger could have been partly to identify Peter, foreshadowing the weapon he drew in the Garden of Gethsemane.[25] There is actually a study sketch Leonardo made for Peter's right arm that supports that explanation."[26]

Was Mary Magdalene married to Jesus?

"So," Matt concluded, "that's pretty much what I found out."

"And you said you hadn't gotten very far," Andrea said.

He shrugged. "How did you do?"

"I got all kinds of research done," she answered, "and feel like I'm just getting started."

"You were going to check out the Mary Magdalene angle, right?" Chris asked.

She nodded. "Especially the claim that she and Jesus were married." She opened the book and read aloud. "Teabing says: 'I won't bore you with the countless references to Jesus and Magdalene's union. That has been explored *ad nauseam* by modern historians.'[27]

"I honestly don't know what he means by 'countless refer-ences,'" she said, "because there aren't any."

"Any?" Matt said.

"Except for a 1983 book called *Holy Blood, Holy Grail* by Michael Baigent, Henry Lincoln, and Richard Leigh, but as far as I can tell, bona fide scholars and historians regard that book as, basically, 'pulp fiction.'"[28]

"Teabing even refers to that book in *The Da Vinci Code*. Did you know that?" Chris offered.

"Really?" Andrea said. "Where?"

"Page two fifty-three. He doesn't mention the authors' names—"

"Wait a minute!" Matt interrupted. "What were their names again?"

"Baigent, Lincoln, and Leigh," Chris said.

Matt laughed. "Oh, that's funny," he said.

"What?" Chris and Andrea asked.

"What's Teabing's first name?" Matt asked.

"Leigh," Chris answered.

"And do you notice anything about the letters in Baigent's name?"

It took only a moment, and Andrea and Chris were answering at the same time: Baigent is an anagram of Teabing.

"Good work, Sweetie!" Andrea said.

Chris nodded slowly. "So that's the author's way of acknowledging Baigent and Leigh's book, by giving his main 'scholar' a name that is a combination of their names."

"Pretty clever," Matt said, smiling.

"Oh, but get this," Andrea added. "Those authors have sued the author of *The Da Vinci Code* for plagiarism."[29]

"So maybe their ideas aren't as widespread as Teabing makes them sound?" Matt asked.

"That fits," Chris said. "If you look at page two fifty-three, you'll notice that Teabing talks about 'exhaustive detail' and 'scores of historians' who know all about the marriage of Jesus and Mary...and then he lists *four* 'history' books."

Andrea and Matt opened their copies to that page and nodded as they saw what Chris was talking about.

"Guess how many of those authors," Chris ventured, "have history degrees?"

The couple looked curiously at Chris, but neither hazarded a guess.

"None. Not one," he answered. "And those are the cream of the crop, as far as the eminent historian Leigh Teabing is concerned!"

"Okay," Matt said, "but what about that one gospel that talked about Jesus and Mary making out? What does *that* tell you?"

Andrea suddenly looked tired. "Not much, it turns out. Teabing clearly thinks that passage from *The Gospel of Phillip* is pretty conclusive. Here's what it says:

> And the companion of the Saviour is Mary Magdalene. Christ loved her more than all the disciples and used to kiss her often on her mouth. The rest of the disciples were offended by it and expressed disapproval. They said to him, 'Why do you love her more than all of us?'[30]

"At first," Andrea continued, "I spent a lot of time getting into Teabing's attempts to prove Jesus' and Mary's marriage by talking about what companion means in Aramaic—when *The Gospel of Phillip* wasn't even written in Aramaic but in Coptic—a late form of Egyptian—and even then was a translation of an earlier text in Greek."[31]

"So Teabing talks like the gospel was written in Aramaic when it wasn't?" Matt asked.

She shrugged. "No way to know. But after going around and around on that point, I came to a realization that I think is more important. If Mary and Jesus were married, why would the disciples even ask Jesus why he loved her more than them?"

She turned to Chris. "Would you ever ask Matt why he loves me more than you?"

"Hah!" Chris exclaimed. "Of course not!"

"And we're not even married yet," Andrea emphasized. "So I went down that road for a while, but eventually, it all came down to this." She opened a new book. "Bart Ehrman, chairman of the Department of Religious Studies at the University of North Carolina at Chapel Hill, says about *The Gospel of Philip*: 'It is difficult to assign a date for this work, but it was probably compiled during the third century.'"[32]

"So...if the main source for a supposed marriage between Mary Magdalene and Jesus is third century and the first-century sources of Matthew, Mark, Luke, and John say nothing about it, which should I give more weight to?"

"Good point," Matt admitted. "But doesn't Teabing also say that it would have been very unusual—maybe even scandalous—for an adult Jewish male like Jesus *not* to be married?"

She nodded. "Yes. He says this:

> The social decorum during that time virtually forbid
> a Jewish man to be unmarried. According to Jewish
> custom, celibacy was condemned....If Jesus were not
> married, at least one of the Bible's gospels would
> have mentioned it and offered some explanation for
> his unnatural state of bachelorhood.[33]

"Now, I almost dismissed that on its face," Andrea said, "because I think it's sort of underhanded to argue from a negative like that."

"What do you mean?" Chris asked.

"It seems a little asinine to say 'the gospels never mention that Jesus wasn't married, so that proves he must have been'!"

"I don't know," Matt said. "I think he's still got a point."

"Something else occurs to me," Chris said. "Teabing thinks Matthew, Mark, Luke, and John are bogus, right? In his mind, they were part of Constantine's propaganda campaign."

"Yeah," Matt said. "So?"

"So how does it make any sense for him to try to prove *any* point from them? He can't have it both ways. If the New Testament Gospels are no more than what Teabing says they are, then they have absolutely no probative value in this case."

"Okay, I get that," Matt agreed.

"Even so," Andrea added, handing both Chris and Matt a document she had printed on her computer. "I spent a lot of time on this point. I found that Jesus' twelve disciples were all adult Jewish males, yet in the four earliest Gospels (Matthew, Mark, Luke, and John), not once is their marital status directly noted or remarked on. The only one of the Twelve whose status—married or single—is even hinted at is Simon Peter, and in his case, it is only because his 'mother-in-law' was healed by Jesus.[34] Peter's wife also gets mention in an early letter to a church (1 Corinthians 9:5) as part of a passage considering a leader's freedom to marry or remain single and to support himself or expect help. Other than that, his wife is never identified, and the marital status of the other disciples is never clarified. But if such silence on singleness in the Gospels is (as Teabing suggests) proof that Jesus was married to Mary Magdalene, that could as easily imply that all but Peter were married to her!"[35]

"Also, Saul of Tarsus, a prominent Jew before his conversion to Christianity, says in 1 Corinthians 7:8 that he was single. He even went on in 1 Corinthians 7 to encourage others to stay single, if possible. The first-century Jewish attitude toward unmarried Jewish males was apparently not as harsh as *The Da Vinci Code* portrays.

"And the first century historian Josephus spoke admiringly of the Essenes, a Jewish sect who 'neither marry wives, nor are desirous to keep servants.'"[36]

Chris set down the paper on the table. "I'm impressed."

"Me, too," Matt said.

"Thank you," she said. "I could give you more examples, but modesty prevents me." She straightened for a moment, her smug expression suddenly turning to surprise. "Oh, I almost forgot. Here's a quote I thought I should conclude with. Dr. Paul Maier, who has apparently spent his whole academic career researching ancient history, says:

> In sober fact, Jesus never wed anyone, but for years sensationalizing scholars and their novelistic popularizers have played the role of doting mothers trying to marry off an eligible son. Now, if there were even one *spark* of evidence from antiquity that Jesus even *may* have gotten married, then as a historian, I would have to weigh this evidence against the *total* absence of such information in either Scripture or the early church traditions. But there is no such spark—*not a scintilla of evidence* (emphasized by the author)—anywhere in historical sources. Even where one might expect to find such claims in the bizarre, second-century, apocryphal gospels—which the Jesus Seminar and other radical voices are trying so desperately to rehabilitate—there is no reference that Jesus ever got married.[37] [original author's emphasis]

Did Jesus command that Mary Magdalene should lead the Church?

"You've both done a great job," Chris said. "I don't know if I can compete with that." He arranged his research materials. "Okay, let's start with Teabing's claims that Jesus intended for Mary Magdalene to lead the church after his departure. He says:

> 'According to these unaltered gospels, it was not *Peter* to whom Christ gave directions with which to establish the Christian Church. It was *Mary Magdalene*...Jesus was the original feminist. He intended for the future of His Church to be in the hands of Mary Magdalene.'[38]

He glanced up from his copy of the book. "First, I just have to mention how incredible it is for Teabing to refer to 'unaltered gospels' when he *dismisses* gospels acknowledged to have been written in the first century and *relies on* a spurious document called *The Gospel of Mary Magdalene.* Here's the passage he quotes:

> And Peter said, 'Did the Saviour really speak with a woman without our knowledge? Are we to turn about and all listen to her? Did he prefer her to us?'

> And Levi answered, 'Peter, you have always been hot-tempered. Now I see you contending against the woman like an adversary. If the Saviour made her worthy, who are you indeed to reject her? Surely the Saviour knows her very well. That is why he loved her more than us.'"[39]

Chris sighed. "So here's the deal: *The Gospel of Mary Magdalene* is *not* part of the Nag Hammadi manuscripts or Dead Sea Scrolls as Teabing seems to imply. There are three fragments that exist. Two from the third century, and one from the fifth century.[40]

"But I want you to notice that there is no reference whatsoever to Jesus having given Mary instructions to start the church or even that Mary claimed to be given them. And Peter is not portrayed as being jealous about Mary being chosen to start the Church; he is just contesting whether or not Mary had been given special revelation from Christ apart from the rest of the disciples—which makes sense because this gospel is a Gnostic gospel, and 'special revelation' is a key element of Gnosticism."[41]

Did Mary Magdalene bear Christ's child?

"Okay," Andrea said. "But it seems to me that the issue of whether Mary was supposed to have been the leader of the early church is more of a side issue. The main question I was hoping you'd research is the claim that Mary and Jesus had a child together."

"You still want me to go into that?" Chris asked. "Because you've already done a great job on the issue of whether they were married."

"Of course we want you to go into that," Matt said. He leaned in, adding in a mock conspiratorial whisper, "Maybe their child was illegitimate!"

Chris rolled his eyes. "All right," he said, shuffling papers and books.

"Here's what Teabing says:

> Not only was Jesus Christ married, but He was a father. My dear, Mary Magdalene was the Holy Vessel. She was the chalice that bore the royal blood-line of Jesus Christ. She was the womb that bore the lineage, and the vine from which the sacred fruit sprang forth![42]

"He goes on to say, of course, that the church covered this up, fearing that Mary, being of the 'House of Benjamin' and 'royal descent,' and Jesus—who was also of royal descent—could form 'a potent political union with the potential of making a legitimate claim to the throne and restoring the line of kings as it was under Solomon.' Proof of all this, of course, is supposedly contained in the 'Sangreal documents,' and 'tens of thousands of pages of information' contained 'in four enormous trunks,' along with other evidence that 'is chronicled in exhaustive detail by scores of historians.'"[43]

"So what about all that?" Andrea asked.

Chris shrugged. "As far as I can tell, everything I've just said—with the exception of Jesus being of royal descent—is total fiction."

"None of it's true?" Andrea asked.

"Not even close," Chris answered. "Concerning Mary's supposed lineage, Professor of Ancient History Paul Maier says that 'there is no record whatsoever of Mary's tribal affiliation.'[44] And I found the whole line of thought about royal blood to be puzzling. The only sense I could make of it is that maybe Teabing figured that if Mary Magdalene could be of the tribe of Benjamin that she and Jesus would have brought the royal lines of King David and King Saul together again. But that has to be pure conjecture because there is no genealogy of Mary Magdalene given anywhere. Apparently, only Teabing knows this supposed 'fact.'"

"But what about all those documents he talks about?" Matt argued. "He can't just be making all that up!"

"Why not?" Chris asked. "It's a novel, remember?"

"But," Matt pressed, "this is a key point in the plotline. If he's been building to a climax only to make stuff up at the key point—"

Chris broke in, "According to Paul Maier, a bona fide scholar of ancient history:

> In fact, there was no such find. No trunks, no docu-
> ments, nor even any search for them by the Knights
> Templar. Furthermore, the Jerusalem Temple—the
> very citadel of Judaism—would be the last place on
> earth to look for *Christian* documents relating to the
> Holy Grail. And even in fiction, Brown cannot pro-
> duce these 'tens of thousands of pages' for us at the
> culmination of his plot."[45]

"But," Matt protested, "there has to be more substance to it than that!"

Chris shook his head. "If you find any, let me know. But you know what I think is the single most intriguing thing about *The Da Vinci Code* phenomenon?"

"What?" Andrea asked, ingenuously.

"Even if the book's central claim about Jesus and Mary being husband and wife and having a child were true, it would mean nothing."

"What are you talking about?" Matt asked.

"It's like this," Chris explained. "Professor Bock told an interviewer,

> If Jesus had been married it wouldn't touch the the-
> ology one bit. Jesus is 100 percent human. Had he

been married and had he had children, all it would
have done would have been to reflect his engage-
ment with his humanity—but I just don't think historically there's any evidence that Jesus was married.
But the important point in relationship to the novel
is, had Jesus been married, the church wouldn't have
had any reason to suppress that knowledge.[46]

"In fact," said Chris, leaning closer, "here's a little tidbit
for you. There actually are millions of Jesus' blood relatives living on earth today. There are probably some in this room." He
looked around the coffee shop as though sharing something
top secret. Then he turned back to Matt and Andrea and whis-
pered, "They're called Jews."

Andrea laughed out loud, and Matt even cracked a smile.

"Not only that," Chris went on, "but while the Bible is
utterly *silent* on whether Jesus married and had children, it is
utterly *clear* that we—*every one* of us, not just blood descen-
dants—can become children of God, adopted into his family
with all the rights and inheritance that children enjoy.[47] To me,
that seems to be a greater mystery than *The Da Vinci Code*."

Is Mary Magdalene the Holy Grail?

"So let me get this straight," Matt said. "There's no reliable
evidence that Jesus intended for Mary Magdalene to lead the
church. There's no reliable evidence that Jesus and Mary were
married. And there's no reliable evidence that they had a child."

Chris locked gazes with his friend. "Yes, I think that is all
true."

"So," said Andrea, "the book's central claim—that the
Holy Grail is not a thing but a *person*—is...bogus?"[48]

Chris nodded. "The Grail legend is just that: a legend. It
has made for some great stories and songs, but even without
Teabing's flights of fancy, there is no reason to expect that the
cup Jesus used at the Last Supper would have any more significance than any other artifact from his life. If the 'Holy Grail'

were found tomorrow, it would make news and be bought for an outrageous price, but it has never had anything to do with the mission or influence of the church."

"So," Matt asked, "what pieces of Teabing's case have turned out to be historically accurate?"

For a moment, the three friends looked blankly at each other.

"Well," Andrea offered, "the Knights Templar and Opus Dei are real."

"But they bear very little resemblance to Teabing's versions," Chris added.

"I've learned a lot," Andrea added, "about the various gospels and when they were written."

"And which ones were reliable," said Matt.

"Not to mention all that stuff about the church fathers, and Constantine and the Council of Nicaea," Andrea said.

"That's true," Chris said. "We've learned a tremendous amount."

Matt nodded slowly. "Yeah," he said. "It hasn't been a waste of time at all."

"I agree," said Chris. "But there's one more thing I'd like to ask you to explore with me."

"What's that?" Andrea asked.

"As we've researched some of Teabing's and Langdon's claims in *The Da Vinci Code*, we've had some stimulating conversations about Jesus, Mary Magdalene, the Bible, and the Church. But the next time we get together, I'd like you to let me lead us down one new avenue of exploration, focused on the answers to two questions: If Jesus wasn't who Sir Leigh Teabing and Robert Langdon say he was, then who was he—really?"

"Okay, sure" said Matt.

"But you said 'two questions,'" Andrea remembered. "What's the other question?"

Chris leveled a serious expression at his two friends. "The other question is this: What difference does it make?"

Chapter Four Notes

1. 2.
2. http://www.louvre.fr.
3. 21.
4. See
   http://www.louvre.or.jp/louvre/presse/en/activites.archives/anniv.htm.
5. 21.
6. "Lillian Schwartz of Bell Labs and Digby quested of the Maudsley Hospital in London." See "Criticisms of *The Da Vinci Code,*" at http://www.wikipedia.org, accessed January 10, 2006.
7. Bruce Boucher, "Does 'The Da Vinci Code' Crack Leonardo?" *New York Times.* August 3, 2003. (www.nytimes.com [archives]).
8. 120-121.
9. 121.
10. 138.
11. Ibid.
12. Boucher, "Does 'The Da Vinci Code' Crack Leonardo?"
13. 2.
4. 236.
15. Ibid.
16. Matthew 26:17-30; Mark 14:12-26; Luke 22:7-38; and John 13:1-30.
17. 243.
18. 244, 245.
19. 1452-1519.
20. Sian Gibby, "Mrs. God," *Slate*, November 3, 2003, (http://www.slate.com/id/2090640).
21. Boucher, "Does 'The Da Vinci Code' Crack Leonardo?"
22. John 13:25.
23. 248.
24. John 13:21-24.
25. Richard Abanes, *The Truth Behind The Da Vinci Code* (Eugene, OR: Harvest House Publishers, 2004), 75.
26. Pietro C. Marani, *Leonardo da Vinci: The Complete Paintings* (New York: Harry N. Abrams, 1999), 231.
27. 247.
28. This book has been soundly debunked in such articles as those found at http://anzwers.org/free/posmis/, http://www.alpheus.org/html/articles/esoteric history/richardson1.html, and http://www.anzwers.org/free/posde-bunking/.)
29. Hugh Davies, "Brown stole idea for Da Vinci Code, claim authors," London News-Telegraph, 10/21/2005. (http://www.telegraph.co.uk/news/main.jhtml?xml=/news /2005 /10/21/wvinci21.xml&sSheet=/news/2005/10/21/ixnewstop.html).
30. 246.
31. Abanes, *Truth Behind Da Vinci*, 39.

32. Bart D. Ehrman, *Lost Scriptures: Books That Did Not Make It Into the New Testament* (New York: Oxford University Press, 2003), 38; A.K. Helmbold, "Nag Hammadi," in Geoffrey W. Broomiley, gen. ed., *The International Standard Bible Encyclopedia* (Grand Rapids, MI: Eerdmans, 1986), 473; and James M. Robinson, *The Nag Hammadi Library* (San Francisco: HarpersSanFrancisco, 1978), 38, 124, 141, and 524.
33. 245.
34. Bock, *Breaking the Da Vinci Code*, 41.
35. Matthew 8:14.
36. Josephus, in *The Works of Flavius Josephus,* 531.
37. Hanegraaff and Maier, *Da Vinci Fact or Fiction,* 16.
38. 248.
39. 247.
40. Karen King, *The Gospel of Mary of Magdala* (Santa Rosa, CA: Polebridge Press, 2003), 16-17.
41. Bock, *Breaking the Da Vinci Code*, 24-25.
42. 249.
43. 248, 249, 256, and 253, respectively.
44. Hanegraaff and Maier, *Da Vinci Code Fact or Fiction*, 18.
45. Ibid, 32.
46. Beliefnet.com article (http://www.beliefnet.com/story/145/story_14506_1/html).
47. John 1:12.
48. 236-238.

Chapter Five
"What Difference Does It Make?"

By the time Chris met Matt and Andrea again, all three had finished *The Da Vinci Code*. They huddled over steaming drinks at their favorite spot and reminisced over favorite parts of the novel. Before long, however, Chris turned the conversation to a more serious subject.

Did later Christians "hijack" Jesus from his earliest followers?

"Let's start here," Chris said. "Teabing says, referring to the time of Constantine, 'Until that moment in history, Jesus was viewed by His followers as a mortal prophet . . . a great and powerful man, but a *man* nonetheless. A mortal.'[1] He adds, 'Many scholars claim that the early Church literally *stole* Jesus from his original followers, hijacking His human message, shrouding it in an impenetrable cloak of divinity, and using it to expand their own power.'[2]

"Do you know who those scholars are?" Chris asked his friends.

Matt and Andrea shook their heads in unison.

"Me neither," Chris said with a smile. "He never says. But the question remains: Did Jesus and his earliest followers actually claim that he was divine? Teabing says no. I say yes.

"Remember, while some scholars disagree as to the precise dating, virtually everyone agrees that the earliest Gospels we have today are Matthew, Mark, Luke, and John. These documents originated shortly after the events they describe and are the primary documents the followers of Christ have viewed as authentic and even inspired since long before the time of Constantine.

"And remember, Jesus and his disciples were all Jews. They were not from a background inclined to call any great individual a god. As Jews, it would have been impressed upon them from the earliest age that there is only one God; it would have been almost unthinkable for them to go around calling anyone divine, no matter how impressive or influential that person may have been. And yet, there are statements or actions by Jesus and his disciples declaring his deity on page after page of the New Testament."

Chris handed each of his friends a page, printed on both sides. The front of the page contained the title, "Jesus claimed to be divine" and listed various New Testament passages.[3] The reverse bore the heading, "Jesus' followers described him as divine," and bore similar excerpts.[4] Matt and Andrea started reading, but Chris interrupted.

"You can look over these later, one by one," he said, "if you're interested. But there can be little doubt, based on the earliest and most reliable evidence, that Jesus' earliest followers—and Jesus himself—saw him as both human and divine. Though Christians and the church have struggled for two millenia to understand that mystery, there's no doubt that even the earliest Christians believed it."

"In other words," Andrea offered, "there was no hijacking."

Chris nodded.

Is there any evidence for Jesus' and his followers' claims?

As Matt set the sheet of paper down on the table, something in his expression prompted Chris to ask, "What? Is something wrong?"

Matt pursed his lips and pointed at the page. "It's just—well, I can accept all that. I mean, these were the earliest Christian writings, at least as far as we know, right?"

"Right," Chris agreed.

"But still, even if Jesus said he was divine and even if his followers said he was, that doesn't mean he *was*. It just means they *said* he was."

"True," Chris said. "But Jesus and his followers didn't just go around claiming that Jesus was God without any evidence at all."

"What sort of evidence did they cite?" Matt asked.

"His virgin birth for one."[5]

Matt looked unimpressed.

"His miracles for another," Chris added.[6]

Matt's expression remained skeptical.

"Remember, the earliest gospels were circulating within the lifetimes of people who had known Jesus and seen the things the gospel writers recorded."

Matt shrugged.

"But I think one of the most compelling kinds of evidence they cited," Chris said, "is the fulfillment of messianic prophecy."[7]

"Fulfillment of what?" Andrea asked.

"Messianic prophecy," Chris explained. "That is, predictions about the Messiah written hundreds of years before Jesus' birth."

"So," Andrea said, "Jesus' followers weren't the first to write about him?"

Chris smiled. "No, they weren't. And it certainly wasn't the Gnostic writers; they tried to add to and reinterpret the eyewitness accounts of the New Testament writers. The first writings about Christ were actually composed hundreds of years—in some cases more than a thousand years—before his birth. The Old Testament, written over a one-thousand-year period, contains over three hundred predictions concerning the coming Messiah, all of which were fulfilled in Jesus of Nazareth."

"Like what?" Matt asked.

"Like that he would be born in the tiny town of Bethlehem, in Judea. Like, um, that he would one day ride into Jerusalem on a donkey colt. That he would be betrayed by a friend—for thirty pieces of silver—and be executed with criminals and buried in a rich man's tomb.[8] And that's just for starters."

"Really," Andrea said. It wasn't a question.

"But, if you ask me, the most important evidence of who Jesus was—and is—is the resurrection."

Was the resurrection of Jesus Christ fact or fiction?

Chris pulled out a stack of papers filled with various notes and excerpts. "It seems to me that either the resurrection of Jesus Christ is one of the *most wicked, vicious, heartless hoaxes ever foisted upon the minds of men,* or it is the most fantastic fact of history.

"The main reason the earliest disciples of Jesus gave for his divinity was the fact that he had actually risen from the dead. Philosopher and New Testament scholar Dr. William Lane Craig writes:

> Without the belief in the resurrection the Christian faith could not have come into being. The disciples would have remained crushed and defeated men. Even had they continued to remember Jesus as their beloved teacher, his crucifixion would have forever silenced any hopes of his being the Messiah. The cross would have remained the sad and shameful end of his career. The origin of Christianity therefore hinges on the belief of the early disciples that God had raised Jesus from the dead.[9]

"The apostle Paul cited Christ's resurrection as absolutely central to the Christian faith. He put it very simply, saying, 'If Christ has not been raised, then our preaching is vain, your faith also is vain... and if Christ has not been raised, your faith is worthless; you are still in your sins.'[10]

"In fact," Chris continued, "Jesus himself predicted his resurrection in an unmistakable and straightforward manner. While his disciples simply couldn't understand it, the Jews took his assertions quite seriously. Listen to what Dr. Bernard Ramm writes:

> Taking the Gospel record as faithful history there can be no doubt that Christ Himself anticipated His death

and resurrection, and plainly declared it to His disciples. . . . The gospel writers are quite frank to admit
that such predictions really did not penetrate their
minds till the resurrection was a fact (John 20:9). But
the evidence is there....He told them that He would
be put to death violently, through the cause of hatred,
and would rise the third day. All this came to pass. [11]

"Over and over again in no uncertain terms, Jesus told his
disciples that he would be raised from the dead." He handed
each of his friends an identical sheet of paper. "This is a list of
where those predictions are recorded; I'd be happy to look
them up any time you want and go over them, one by one, if
you're interested." The sheet listed:

- Matthew 12:38–40; 16:21; 17:9; 17:22, 23; 20:18, 19; 26:32;
  27:63
- Mark 8:31–9:1; 9:10; 9:31; 10:32–34; 14:28, 58
- Luke 9:22–27
- John 2:18–22; 12:34; chapters 14–16.

"But again," Matt interjected, "I come back to the point I
made earlier. Even if Jesus said it and his earliest followers said
it, doesn't mean it happened."

Chris nodded. "But, in the case of the resurrection, we
have an actual historical claim that can be investigated like any
other event of history. It can't be proven the way a scientific
fact can be proven—in a laboratory, for example—but it can be
investigated and examined much like any historical fact."

Matt jumped in. "From things like letters and portraits
and documents."

"Exactly," Chris agreed. "Historical evidence can help us
discover the truth about Jesus." He lifted a thick book out of
the pile next to him and set it before Matt and Andrea.[12] "This
book contains eighty-two pages of detailed evidence of the
resurrection of Jesus. But let me summarize.

"The four earliest historical documents we possess all
describe the death, burial, and resurrection of Jesus in great

detail," he said.[13] "The vast majority of scholars agree that these documents were written and circulated within the lifetimes of those who witnessed the events and of those who could have refuted any parts that weren't accurate.

"And no one really disputes the fact that the disciples of Jesus began preaching the news of his resurrection soon after the event itself; in fact, Peter's Pentecost sermon in Acts two occurred *within fifty days* of the resurrection. And textual research indicates that the written accounts of the resurrection—especially the creedal statement of first Corinthians fifteen—are astoundingly early in origin, possibly within *two years* of the event!"[14]

"Creedal statement?" Andrea asked.

"Oh, sorry," Chris said. He fished his Bible from his hip pocket. "I got carried away. Many scholars think this is the earliest Christian creed—a summary statement of faith that Christians would recite." He read:

> I passed on to you the most important points of doctrine that I had received:
>
> Christ died to take away our sins as the Scriptures predicted.
>
> He was placed in a tomb.
>
> He was brought back to life on the third day as the Scriptures predicted.
>
> He appeared to Cephas. Next he appeared to the twelve apostles. Then he appeared to more than 500 believers at one time. (Most of these people are still living, but some have died.)[15]

"New Testament scholar Dr. William Lane Craig says this creed 'undoubtedly goes back to within a few years of Jesus' crucifixion.'"[16]

"Okay," Matt allowed, "so the story started very early. That doesn't mean it's true."

Chris nodded. "But the historical evidence," he said, patting the thick book on the table, "strongly attests to its truth.

That's why, shortly after the events themselves, Paul could make that comment about more than five hundred people—most of whom were still around—who had seen the resurrected Jesus!"

Chris picked a photocopied sheet of paper from his notes. "Listen to what Dr. J. N. D. Anderson writes:

> The most drastic way of dismissing the evidence would be to say that these stories were mere fabrications, that they were pure lies. But, so far as I know, not a single critic today would take such an attitude. In fact, it would really be an impossible position. Think of the number of witnesses, over 500. Think of the character of the witnesses, men and women who gave the world the highest ethical teaching it has ever known, and who even on the testimony of their enemies lived it out in their lives. Think of the psychological absurdity of picturing a little band of defeated cowards cowering in an upper room one day and a few days later transformed into a company that no persecution could silence—and then attempting to attribute this dramatic change to nothing more convincing than a miserable fabrication they were trying to foist upon the world. That simply wouldn't make sense.[17]

"And Dr. John Warwick Montgomery comments:

> Note that when the disciples of Jesus proclaimed the resurrection, they did so as eyewitnesses and they did so while people were still alive who had had contact with the events they spoke of. In A.D. 56 Paul wrote that over 500 people had seen the risen Jesus and that most of them were still alive (1 Corinthians 15:6ff.). It passes the bounds of credibility that the early Christians could have manufactured such a tale and then preached it among those who might easily

have refuted it simply by producing the body of Jesus.[18]

"And—I'll end with this—Oxford historian Thomas Arnold, author of the famous three-volume *History of Rome*, said:

> Thousands and tens of thousands of persons have gone through [the evidence for the resurrection] piece by piece, as carefully as every judge summing up on a most important cause. I have myself done it many times over, not to persuade others but to satisfy myself. I have been used for many years to study the histories of other times, and to examine and weigh the evidence of those who have written about them, and I know of no one fact in the history of mankind which is proved by better and fuller evidence of every sort, to the understanding of a fair inquirer, than the great sign which God hath given us that Christ died and rose again from the dead.[19]

What difference does it make?

Andrea drained her cup as Chris finished reading. Matt chewed his lip, slowly.

"Okay," Matt said, "that makes sense. But I just can't believe it. I think it's more realistic to respect Jesus as a great teacher, like it says in *The Da Vinci Code*."

Chris leaned back in his chair. "I don't think Jesus left that option open to you."

Matt's jaw dropped. "What did you say?"

"I don't think Jesus left that option open to you. Or me. Or anyone. You see, according to the historical record, Jesus apparently thought it was critical what others believed about him. It was not a subject that allowed for neutrality."

"I think we've already seen that the New Testament books are reliable historical records; so reliable, in fact, that Jesus cannot be dismissed as a mere legend. There is every reason to believe that the earliest gospel accounts preserve an accurate record of the things he did, the places he visited, and the words he spoke. And they make it clear that Jesus definitely claimed to be God. So every person must answer the question: Is his claim to deity true or false?"

Matt shifted nervously in his chair, but Chris kept going. "In the first century, when people were giving a number of answers about Jesus' identity, Jesus asked His disciples, 'But who do you say that I am?' to which Peter responded, 'You are the Christ, the Son of the living God.'[20] Not everyone accepts Peter's answer, but no one should avoid Jesus' question.

"Jesus' claim to be God—which his earliest followers claimed was certified by the fact of his resurrection—must be either true or false. If Jesus' claims to be God were false, then there are just two options."

Was he a liar?

"Let's suppose," Chris said, focusing on Andrea, "that when Jesus claimed to be God, he knew he was not God. What would you say about him then?"

"I'd say he was a liar," she answered.

Chris nodded. "I would, too. In fact, if he was a liar, then he was also a hypocrite because he told others to be honest, whatever the cost...while he, at the same time, was teaching and living a colossal lie.

"More than that, I'd have to say he was a demon because he deliberately told others to trust him for their eternal destiny. If he knew his claims were false—knowing also that he could not back up his claims, then he was unspeakably evil in deliberately misleading so many followers down through the centuries."

Andrea nodded. "I can see that."

"Last," Chris said, "he would also be a fool because it was his claims to deity that led to his own crucifixion—a pretty predictable conclusion in that day and age.

"So, if Jesus was a liar, a con man, and, therefore, an evil, foolish man, then how can we explain the fact that he left us with the most profound moral instruction and powerful moral example anyone has ever given? Could a deceiver, an imposter of monstrous proportions, teach such unselfish ethical truths and live such a morally exemplary life as Jesus did?"

Andrea didn't answer. Matt listened impassively.

Was he a lunatic?

"Okay," Chris continued. "So maybe it's inconceivable for Jesus to have been a liar. Maybe it's unthinkable that he knew he wasn't God and yet told people he was anyway. But there is another possibility." He paused.

Andrea was thoroughly engaged in the flow of Chris' logic. "He could have sincerely thought he was God."

Chris nodded. "He could have been completely sincere...but wrong." Another pause. "But what would you think of me if you believed I was sincere in believing I was God?"

"Crazy." It was Matt's first word since refilling his coffee cup.

Chris nodded, smiling at Matt. "Especially someone in a fiercely monotheistic culture—who goes around telling others that their eternal destiny depends on believing in him."

He pulled a photocopied sheet from his notes. "Philosopher Peter Kreeft has some great comments about this possibility:

> A measure of your insanity is the size of the gap between what you think you are and what you really are. If I think I am the greatest philosopher in America, I am only an arrogant fool; if I think I am Napoleon, I am probably over the edge; if I think I am a butterfly, I am fully embarked from the sunny shores of sanity. But if I think I am God, I am even more insane because the gap between anything finite and the infinite God is even greater than the

gap between any two finite things, even a man and a butterfly.

. . . Well, then, why [was Jesus not a] liar or lunatic? . . . [A]lmost no one who has read the Gospels can honestly and seriously consider that option. The savviness, the canniness, the human wisdom, the attractiveness of Jesus emerge from the Gospels with unavoidable force to any but the most hardened and prejudiced reader. . . . Compare Jesus with liars . . . or lunatics like the dying Nietzsche. Jesus has in abundance precisely those three qualities that liars and lunatics most conspicuously lack: (1) his practical wisdom, his ability to read human hearts; (2) his deep and winning love, his passionate compassion, his ability to attract people and make them feel at home and forgiven, his authority, "not as the scribes"; (3) his ability to astonish, his unpredictability, his creativity. Liars and lunatics are all so dull and predictable! No one who knows both the Gospels and human beings can seriously entertain the possibility that Jesus was a liar or a lunatic, a bad man."[21]

He is Lord!

Chris reached to the table for a book and opened it. "C. S. Lewis," he continued, "the great professor of English literature at Cambridge University and a former agnostic, said this in his book *Mere Christianity*:

I am trying here to prevent anyone saying the really foolish thing that people often say about Him: 'I'm ready to accept Jesus as a great moral teacher, but I don't accept His claim to be God.' That is the one thing we must not say. A man who was merely a man and said the sort of things Jesus said would not be a great moral teacher. He would either be a lunatic—on a level with the man who says he is a poached egg—or else he would be the Devil of Hell. You must make your choice. Either this man was, and is, the Son of God: or else a mad man or something worse. You can shut Him up for a fool, you can spit at Him and kill Him as a demon; or you can fall at His feet and call Him Lord and God. But let us not come up with any patronizing nonsense about His being a great human teacher. He has not left that open to us. He did not intend to.[22]

"If Jesus of Nazareth is not a liar or a lunatic, then he must be Lord...which was certainly the conclusion of those who knew him best, those who experienced his love, his forgiveness, and his power to live their lives on a new level."

Suddenly Andrea, wide-eyed, reached out and grabbed her boyfriend's arm. "Whoa, wait—wait a minute," she said.

"What?" Matt asked.

Chris and Matt stared at her while long moments passed.

Finally, she spoke. "If all this is really true, then...then that means it's real."

"What do you mean?" Matt asked.

She lifted her hands to her head and massaged her temples. "Let's see if I can express what I'm thinking. When Chris talked about God's love and forgiveness, that's what made me realize it. See, it's like, this isn't about people who lived two thousand years ago, or even about a code created by a renaissance genius; it's about—well, it's about me. I mean, think about it, Matt! If it's not true, then all God says about love and forgiveness and so on isn't real." She looked from Matt to Chris, as though expecting one of them to complete her thought. "But if it is true...then it's real. Really real. All of it."

"All of what?" Matt asked.

Her eyes clouded with tears. "That God loves you. That he's willing to forgive you, and accept you, and—" She turned to Chris. "Right?"

Chris nodded solemnly. "Right," he said. "If it's true, then it's real. Everything God says about who he is, and who you are, and what he is willing to do for you....What he has already done for you."

"That's the answer," Matt said.

"The answer?" Andrea asked.

"To what Chris said he wanted to talk to us about," Matt responded. "That's the answer to the question: What difference does it make?"

"Yeah," Chris agreed. "Exactly."

Chapter Five Notes

1. 233.
2. Ibid.
3. See Matthew 28:18-20; Mark 2:5-7; Luke 23:42-43; John 5:23, 24; John 8:19; John 8:58-59; John 14:1; John 14:6-11; John 19:7; and John 10:29-34, among others.
4. See John 20:28 (Thomas); John 1:1-14 and 1 John 5:20 (John); Romans 9:5, Philippians 2:6-11, and Colossians 1:15-17 (Paul), as well as Paul's benediction of 2 Corinthians 13:14, which equates the Father, Son, and Holy Spirit.
5. For an elucidation of the evidential value of the virgin birth, see *Beyond Belief to Convictions* by Josh McDowell and Bob Hostetler (Wheaton, IL: Tyndale House Publishers, 2002), 68-71.
6. For an elucidation of the evidential value of Jesus' miracles, see *Beyond Belief to Convictions* by Josh McDowell and Bob Hostetler, 71-77.
7. For an elucidation of these prophecies, see *The New Evidence that Demands a Verdict* by Josh McDowell (Nashville: Thomas Nelson Publishers, 1993), 164-202.
8. Micah 5:2; Matthew 2:1; Zechariah 9:9; Matthew 21:2; Psalm 41:9; Matthew 26:49; Zechariah 11:12; Matthew 26:15; Isaiah 53:12; Matthew 27:38; Isaiah 53:9; and Matthew 27:57-60.
9. William Lane Craig, *Knowing the Truth about the Resurrection* (Ann Arbor, MI: Servant Books, 1988), 116-17.
10. 1 Corinthians 15:14, 17.
11. Bernard Ramm, *Protestant Christian Evidences* (Chicago: Moody Press, 1953), 191.
12. McDowell, *New Evidence that Demands a Verdict*
13. Matthew 27:1-28:15; Mark 15:1-16:8; Luke 22:66-24:49; and John 19:1-21:14.
14. Lee Strobel, *The Case for Christ* (Grand Rapids, MI: Zondervan Publishing House, 1998), 230.
15. 1 Corinthians 15:3-6, GWT.
16. Lee Strobel, *The Case for Easter* (Grand Rapids, MI: Zondervan Publishing House, 1998, 2003), 36.
17. J.N.D. Anderson, "The Resurrection of Jesus Christ." *Christianity Today,* March 29, 1968, 5-6.
18. John W. Montgomery, *History and Christianity* (Downers Grove, IL: InterVarsity Press, 1971), 78.
19. Thomas Arnold, as cited in Wilbur Smith's *Therefore Stand* (Grand Rapids, MI: Baker Book House, 1945), 425-26.
20. Matthew 16:15, 16, NIV.
21. Peter Kreeft, *Fundamentals of the Faith: Essays in Christian Apologetics* (San Francisco: Ignatius Press, 1988), 60 and 61.
22. C.S. Lewis, *Mere Christianity* (New York: Macmillan, 1952), 40 and 41.

Chapter Six
A Quest Fulfilled

"There is within every soul a thirst for happiness and meaning."
—*Thomas Aquinas*

Dan Brown's novel, *The Da Vinci Code*, depicts a fictional quest by fictional characters for a fictional Holy Grail. It has sold millions of copies not only because it's an entertaining book but also because every one of us is on a quest, and we long to discover the secret and fulfill our quest—though we may not even know what we're looking for, really.

Although the characters in this book, Chris, Matt, and Andrea, are also fictional characters, the details of their discussions are factual, and the hundreds of cited references in their conversations provide not only the factual underpinnings but also the opportunity for you to further investigate their claims and discoveries.

And, along with them, our common quest isn't about people who lived two thousand years ago or even about a code created by a renaissance genius; it's about much bigger things than that. It's about who God is, who Jesus is, who we are—and whether or not the things God says about love and forgiveness and salvation are actually real.

Who God is...
Some folks believe it doesn't matter whether the Gospels are accurate or whether Jesus is fully human and fully divine or whether Jesus really rose from the dead. But it does matter. Because if these things are true, then—as Andrea said—the love of God and the wonderful plans he has for you are real! If those things are true, then God really does exist. If those things are true, then Jesus really died out of love for you. If those things are true, then you really can be forgiven, and your

past can be washed clean. If those things are true, then you really can know God intimately. If those things are true, then you really can experience God's unconditional love and acceptance. If those things are true, then you really can fulfill God's wildest dreams for your life.

The Christian faith is not about finding (or suppressing) some secret knowledge or learning some long-hidden secrets about Jesus. In fact, there's no secret to it. God in His great love desires for each of us to enjoy a relationship with Him. He's been pretty clear about that since the days of Moses, who said: "You must worship no other gods, but only the LORD, for he is a God who is passionate about his relationship with you" (Exodus 34:14, NLT).

Who Jesus is...

God wants to walk with us and give us the joy of participating in what He is already doing. Our common search for answers is about taking what God has revealed about Himself, through the life of His Son, Jesus Christ, and based upon that revelation, making a decision of faith to follow Him. Our faith becomes obedience which turns into joy and praise as we see God do things we never dreamed possible in our lives.

How does one get to know Him like that? Is it even possible to know God personally or to find real answers to such important questions?

Who we are and what God says about love and forgiveness and salvation...

It is possible to know God in an intimate, personal way—to find meaning and purpose in life and to find not a truth but *the* truth.

I know because God changed me, a former staunch skeptic of the Bible, of religion, and of Jesus Christ Himself. In my quest to find happiness and meaning for my life, as well as to accept a challenge posed to me by college peers who were

Christians, I worked for months, assembling data, and weighing evidence. In fact, I left the university I was attending and traveled to Europe to study and gather research to prove that there were no intellectual grounds for believing in Jesus Christ.

Then one day, after much research, while I was sitting in a library in London, England, it was as though God was saying to me, "Josh, you don't have a leg to stand on." I immediately suppressed it. Still, just about every day after that I heard the same inner voice, and the more I researched, the more I heard this voice.

I returned to the United States and to the university, but I couldn't sleep at night. I would go to bed at ten o'clock and lie awake until four in the morning, trying to refute the overwhelming evidence I was accumulating that Jesus Christ was God's Son.

I began to realize that I was being intellectually dishonest. My mind told me that the claims of Christ were indeed true, but my will was being pulled another direction. I began to sense Christ's personal challenge to me in Revelation 3:20: "Here I am! I stand at the door and knock. If anyone hears my voice and opens the door, I will come in and eat with him, and he with me" (NIV). But becoming a Christian seemed so ego-shattering to me. I had placed so much emphasis on finding the truth, but I wasn't willing to follow it once I saw it.

I knew I had to resolve this inner conflict because it was driving me crazy. I had always considered myself an open-minded person, so I decided to put Christ's claims to the supreme test. One night at my home in Union City, Michigan, at the end of my second year at the university, I became a Christian. Someone may say, "How do you *know* you became a Christian?" I was there! I got alone with a Christian friend and prayed four things that established my relationship with God and changed my life forever.

For you, the circumstances may be different from the way He worked in my life, but the same truth, the one and only truth, that transformed my life and satisfied my longing heart and searching mind will do the same for you. God has a different plan for each individual, but He, nevertheless, wants us all to experience the same fullness of joy.

Let me encourage you to take a moment to read over this last short section. If you follow through on what you read, I guarantee your life will be changed forever.

1. Can we really know God personally...

- God **loves** you and created you to know Him personally. "God so loved the world, that He gave His only begotten Son, that whoever believes in Him should not perish, but have eternal life" (John 3:16).
- God has a plan for **you.** "Now this is eternal life: that they may know you, the only true God, and Jesus Christ, whom you have sent" (John 17:3, NIV).

2. What prevents us from knowing Him personally...

- Humans are **sinful**. "All have sinned and fall short of the glory of God" (Romans 3:23).

     Although we were created to have fellowship with God, because of our own stubborn self-will, we choose to go our own independent way and fellowship with God has been broken. This self-will, characterized by an attitude of active rebellion or passive indifference, is an evidence of what the Bible calls sin.

- Humans are **separated**. "The wages of sin is death" [spiritual separation from God] (Romans 6:23). "...(Those) who do not know God and do not obey the gospel of our Lord Jesus...will be punished with everlasting destruction and shut out from the presence of the Lord..." (2 Thessalonians 1:8,9).

     This sin, which is manifested in each of our individual lives, separates us from God's love and from an intimate relationship with Him. Such separation brings both earthly turmoil and eternal consequences.

3. God provided a way to bridge this separation...

Jesus Christ, God's Son, is God's **only** provision for man's sin. Through Him alone, we can know God personally and experience His love.

- **Christ Died in Our Place**—"God demonstrates His own love toward us, in that while we were yet sinners, Christ died for us" (Romans 5:8).
- **Christ Rose From the Dead**—"Christ died for our sins...He was buried...He was raised on the third day according to the Scriptures...He appeared to Peter, then to the twelve. After that He appeared to more than five hundred..." (1 Corinthians 15:3-6).
- **Christ is the Only Way to God**—"Jesus said to him, 'I am the way, and the truth, and the life; no one comes to the Father, but through Me'" (John 14:6).

But...

4. It is not enough just to know these truths...

- We must individually **receive** Jesus Christ as Savior and Lord; then we can know God personally and experience His love. *"As many as received Him, to them He gave the right to become children of God, even to those who believe in His name" (John 1:12).*
- We receive Christ through faith, placing our trust in Him, His power and authority. *"By grace you have been saved through faith; and that not of yourselves, it is the gift of God; not as a result of works that no one should boast" (Ephesians 2:8,9).*
- We receive Christ by the power of the Holy Spirit. *"No one can say, "Jesus is Lord, except by the Holy Spirit." (1 Corinthians 12:3).*

And...

5. **When we receive Christ..**
   - We receive Him by faith and experience a new birth (John 3:1-8).

   Receiving Christ involves turning to God from self (repentance) and trusting Christ to come into our lives to forgive us of our sins and to make us what He wants us to be. Just to agree intellectually that Jesus Christ is the Son of God and that He died on the cross for our sins is not enough, nor is it enough to have an emotional experience.

6. **The Bible promises eternal life to all who receive Christ...**
   - When we receive Him, we are assured to have eternal life in heaven and abundant, meaningful life even here on earth. "The witness is this, that God has given us eternal life, and this life is in His Son. He who has the Son has the life; he who does not have the Son of God does not have the life. These things I have written to you who believe in the name of the Son of God, in order that you may know that you have eternal life" (1 John 5:11-13).

A departing word...

Even right now, you can pray to Christ and receive him through faith. The words of the following prayer are not magical but simply a suggestion to express a sincere desire to turn from self and to turn to God:

"Lord Jesus, I believe that you are who you claimed to be, and I want to know You personally. Thank You for dying on the cross for my sins. I open the door of my life and receive You as my Savior and Lord. Thank You for forgiving me of my sins and giving me eternal life. Take control of my life. Make me the kind of person You want me to be."

If you prayed the above prayer with a genuine desire to receive Christ, thank God often that Christ is in your life, that He will never leave you (Hebrews 13:5), and that He has called you to embark upon an exciting life journey with Him, the true answer to your quest.

The Da Vinci Code: A Quest for Answers

Bibliography

Abanes, Richard. *The Truth Behind The Da Vinci Code*. Eugene: Harvest House Publishers, 2004.

Addison. *The History of the Knights Templars, the Temple Church, and the Temple*, 3rd ed, 1852. New York: AMS Press reprint, 1978.

Albright, W. F. *The Archaeology of Palestine*, rev. Baltimore: Penguin Books, 1960.

Albright, W. F. *Recent Discoveries in Bible Lands*. New York: Funk and Wagnalls, 1955.

Anderson, J. N. D. "The Resurrection of Jesus Christ." *Christianity Today*, March 29, 1968.

Archer, Gleason L. *Encyclopedia of Bible Difficulties*. Grand Rapids: Zondervan Publishing House, 1982.

Arndt, William F., and F. Wilbur Gingrich. *A Greek-English Lexicon of the New Testament and Other Early Christian Literature*. Chicago: The University of Chicago Press, 1952.

Athanasius. *Letters*, no. 39 (Easter 367). In *A Select Library of the Nicene and Post-Nicene Fathers of the Christian Church*. vol. 4 by Philip Schaff, ed. New York: The Christian Literature Company, 1888.

Barber, Malcolm. "The Trial of the Templars Revisited" in *The Military Orders: Welfare and Warfare* by H. Nicolson, ed. Aldershot, England: Ashgate, 1998.

Blaiklock, Edward Musgrave. *The Acts of the Apostles*. Grand Rapids: William B. Eerdmans Publishing Co., 1959.

Blaiklock, Edward Musgrave. *Layman's Answer: An Examination of the New Theology*. London: Hodder and Stoughton, 1968.

Bloomberg, Craig. "The Da Vinci Code", *Denver Seminary Journal* (2004), vol. 7. (www.denverseminary.edu/dj/articles2004/0200/0202.php accessed 9/19/05).

Bock, Darrell L. *Breaking the Da Vinci Code*. Nashville: Thomas Nelson Publishers, 2004.

Boucher, Bruce. "Does 'The Da Vinci Code' Crack Leonardo?" *New York Times*. August 3, 2003. (View at www.nytimes.com [archives].)

Brown, Dan. *The Da Vinci Code*. New York: Doubleday, 2003.

Bruce, F. F. "Archaeological Confirmation of the New Testament." In *Revelation and the Bible*, ed. Carl Henry. Grand Rapids: Baker Book House, 1969.

—. *The Books and the Parchments: How We Got Our English Bible*. Old Tappan, N.J.: Fleming H. Revell Co., 1950. Reprints: 1963, 1984.

—. *The Canon of Scripture*. Downers Grove, Ill.: InterVarsity Press, 1988.

—. *The Defense of the Gospel in the New Testament*. rev. ed. Grand Rapids: Wm. B. Eerdmans, 1977.

—. *Jesus and Christian Origins Outside the New Testament*. Grand Rapids: William B. Eerdmans Publishing Co., 1974.

—. *The New Testament Documents: Are They Reliable?* Downers Grove; IL: InterVarsity Press, 1964.

Burrows, Millar. *The Dead Sea Scrolls*. New York: Viking Press, 1955.

Burrows, Millar. *What Mean These Stones?* New York: Meridian Books, 1957.

Campbell, G. A. *The Knights Templar: A New History*. Stroud, UK: Sutton, 2001.

Case Study: The European Witch-Hunts, c. 1450-1750 and Witch-Hunts Today. http://www.gendercide.org/case_witch-hunts.html

Clouse, Robert G. "Templars" in *The New International Dictionary of the Christian Church* by J. D. Douglas, gen. ed., Grand Rapids: Zondervan, 1974; 1978 ed.

Craig, William Lane. "Did Jesus Rise from the Dead?" *Jesus Under Fire: Modern Scholarship Reinvents the Historical Jesus*. ed. by Michael J. Wilkins and J. P. Moreland. Grand Rapids: Zondervan Publishing House, 1995.

Craig, William Lane. *Knowing the Truth about the Resurrection*. Ann Arbor, Mich.: Servant Books, 1988. Rev. ed. of *The Son Rises*. Chicago: Moody Bible Institute, 1981.

Cuhulian, Kerr. *Full Contact Magick: A Book of Shadows for the Wiccan Warrior*. St. Paul, MN: Llewellyn Publications, 2002.

Currie, George. *The Military Discipline of the Romans from the Founding of the City to the Close of the Republic*. An abstract of a thesis published under the auspices of the Graduate Council of Indiana University, 1928.

Davidson, Samuel. *The Hebrew Text of the Old Testament*. London, 1856.

Earle, Ralph. *How We Got Our Bible*. Grand Rapids: Baker Book House, 1971.

Edersheim, Alfred. *The Life and Times of Jesus the Messiah*. vol. II. Grand Rapids: William B. Eerdmans Publishing Co., 1962.

Edersheim, Alfred. *The Temple: Its Ministry and Services*. Grand Rapids: William B. Eerdmans Publishing Co., 1958.

Edwards, William D., M.D., et al. "On the Physical Death of Jesus Christ," *Journal of the American Medical Association* 255:11. March 21, 1986.

Ehrman, Bart D. *Lost Scriptures: Books That Did Not Make It Into the New Testament*. New York: Oxford University Press, 2003.

Elliger, Karl, and Wilhelm Rudolph, eds., *Biblia Hebraica Stuttgartensia / quae antea cooperantibus A. Alt, O. Eissfeldt, P. Kahle ediderat R. Kittel; editio funditus renovata, adjuvantibus H. Bardtke ... [et al.] cooperantibus H.P. Rüger et J. Ziegler ediderunt K. Elliger et W. Rudolph; textum Masoreticum curavit H.P. Rüger, Masoram elaboravit G.E. Weil; editio tertia emendata opera W. Rudolph et H.P Rüger.* Stuttgart: Deutsche Bibelgesellschaft, 1987.

Ewert, David. *From Ancient Tablets to Modern Translations: A General Introduction to the Bible*. Grand Rapids: Zondervan, 1983.

Ferguson, Everett. "Factors Leading to the Selection and Closure of the New Testament Canon" in *The Canon Debate* by Lee Martin McDonald and James A. Sanders, eds. Peabody, Mass: Hendrickson Publishers, 2002.

Finley, M. I. and H. W. Pleket. *The Olympic Games: The First Thousand Years*. New York: Viking, 1976.

Fisher, J. T., and L. S. Hawley. *A Few Buttons Missing*. Philadelphia, Penn.: Lippincott, 1951.

Free, Joseph P. *Archaeology and Bible History*. Wheaton: Scripture Press, 1969.

Geisler, Norman L., and William E. Nix. *A General Introduction to the Bible*. Chicago: Moody Press, 1968.

Geisler, Norman L. *Baker Encyclopedia of Christian Apologetics.* Grand Rapids: Baker, 1998.

Glueck, Nelson. *Rivers in the Desert: History of Negev.* New York: Farrar, Straus, and Cadahy, 1959.

Gordon, Richard. *Image and Value in the Greco-Roman World.* Aldershot, UK: Variorum, 1996.

Green, Michael. *Man Alive.* Downers Grove, Ill.: InterVarsity Press, 1968.

Greenleaf, Simon. *The Testimony of the Evangelists, Examined by the Rules of Evidence Administered in Courts of Justice.* Grand Rapids: Baker Book House, 1965 (reprinted from 1847 edition).

Greer, John Michael. *The New Encyclopedia of the Occult.* St. Paul, MN: Llewellyn Publications, 2003.

Grimassi, Raven. *Encyclopedia of Wicca & Witchcraft.* St. Paul, MN: Llewellyn Publications, 2000.

Grounds, Vernon C. *The Reason for Our Hope.* Chicago: Moody Press, 1945.

Guttman, Allen. *The Olympics: A History of the Modern Games.* Urbana, IL: University of Illinois Press, 1992.

Habermas, Gary R. *The Verdict of History: Conclusive Evidence for the Life of Jesus.* Nashville: Thomas Nelson Publishers, 1988.

Hanegraaff, Hank, and Paul L. Maier. *The Da Vinci Code: Fact or Fiction?* Wheaton: Tyndale House Publishers, Inc., 2004.

Hanson, George. *The Resurrection and the Life.* London: William Clowes & Sons, Ltd., 1911.

Hartzler, H. Harold. "Foreword." cited in *Science Speaks,* Peter W. Stoner. Chicago: Moody Press, 1963.

Hastings, James, John A. Selbie, and John C. Lambert, eds. *A Dictionary of Christ and the Gospels*. vol. II. New York: Charles Scribner's Sons, 1909.

Helmbold, A. K. "Nag Hammadi" in *The International Standard Bible Encyclopedia* by Geoffrey W. Broomiley, gen. ed.. Grand Rapids: Eerdmans, 1986; 1990 ed.

Henry, B., and R. Yeoman. *An Approved History of the Olympic Games*. Sherman Oaks, CA: Alfred, 1984.

Henry, Carl, ed. *Revelation and the Bible*. Grand Rapids: Baker Book House, 1969.

Hoehner, Harold. *Chronological Aspects of the Life of Christ*. Grand Rapids: Zondervan Publishing House, 1977.

Holloman, Henry W. *An Exposition of the Post-Resurrection Appearances of Our Lord*. Unpublished Th.M. thesis, Dallas Theological Seminary, May 1967.

Hort, Fenton John Anthony, and Brooke Foss Westcott. *The New Testament in the Original Greek*. Vol. 1. New York: Macmillan Co., 1881.

Hort, F. J. A. *Way, Truth and the Life*. New York: Macmillan and Co., 1894.

Ignatius. "Epistle to the Ephesians," in *Genuine Epistles of the Apostolical Fathers* by William of Canterbury, trans. London: Samuel Bagster, 1840.

Josephus, Flavius. "Against Apion," *The Antiquities of the Jews*. New York: Ward, Lock, Bowden & Co., 1900.

—-. *The Antiquities of the Jews*. New York: Ward, Lock, Bowden & Co., 1900.

Kenyon, Frederic G. *The Bible and Archaeology*. New York: Harper & Row, 1940.

—. *Handbook to the Textual Criticism of the New Testament*. London: Macmillan and Company, 1901.

Kieran, J., and A. Dailey. *The Story of the Olympic Games*. Philadelphia: Lippincott, 1977.

King, Karen L. *The Gospel of Mary of Magdala*. Santa Rosa, CA: Polebridge Press, 2003.

Kreeft, Peter. *Fundamentals of the Faith: Essays in Christian Apologetics*. San Francisco: Ignatius Press, 1988.

Kulman, Linda, and Jay Tolson (with Katy Kelly). "Jesus in America," *U.S. News and World Report*, December 22, 2003. (www.usnews.com [archives])

Latham, Henry. *The Risen Master*. Cambridge: Deighton, Bell, and Co., 1904.

Latourette, Kenneth Scott. *A History of Christianity*. New York: Harper and Row, 1953.

Lecky, William Edward Hatpole. *History of European Morals from Augustus to Charlemagne*. New York: D. Appleton and Co., 1903.

Lewis, C. S. *Mere Christianity*. New York: Macmillan, 1952.

Lewis, C. S. *Miracles: A Preliminary Study*. New York: Macmillan, 1947.

Little, Paul E. *Know Why You Believe*. Wheaton: Scripture Press, 1987.

The Lost Books of the Bible and The Forgotten Books of Eden, Cleveland: World Publishing Company, 1926.

Lucian of Samosata. *"Death of Pelegrine."* In *The Works of Lucian of Samosata*, 4 vols. by H. W. Fowler and F. G. Fowler, trans. Oxford: The Clarendon Press, 1949.

Lutzer, Erwin W. *The Da Vinci Deception*. Wheaton: Tyndale House Publishers, Inc. 2004.

Marani, Pietro C. *Leonardo da Vinci: The Complete Paintings*. New York: Harry N. Abrams, Inc., 1999; 2003 ed.

McDowell, Josh. *A Ready Defense: The Best of Josh McDowell*. Nashville: Thomas Nelson Publishers, 1993.

McDowell, Josh. *The New Evidence That Demands a Verdict*. Nashville: Thomas Nelson Publishers, 1999.

McDowell, Josh and Bob Hostetler. *Beyond Belief to Convictions*. Wheaton, IL: Tyndale House Publishers, 2002.

Metzger, Bruce M. "Mystery Religions and Early Christianity" in *Historical and Literary Studies*. Leiden, Netherlands: E. J. Brill, 1968.

Metzger, Bruce M. *The Text of the New Testament*. New York: Oxford University Press, 1968.

Miller, Laura. "The Da Vinci Con," *The New York Times Book Review* (Sunday, February 22, 2004), 23.

Montgomery, John W. *History and Christianity*. Downers Grove, Ill.: InterVarsity Press, 1971.

Moreland, J. P. *Scaling the Secular City*. Grand Rapids: Baker, 1987.

Moyer, Elgin S. *Who Was Who in Church History*, rev. ed. Chicago: Moody Press, 1968.

Nash, Ronald. *Christianity and the Hellenistic World*. Grand Rapids: Zondervan Publishing House, 1984.

Noll, Mark A., *Turning Points: Decisive Moments in the History of Christianity*, Grand Rapids: Baker Book House, 1997.

Payne, J. Barton. *Encyclopedia of Biblical Prophecy*. London: Hodder and Stoughton, 1973.

Pliny the Younger. *Letters*, by W. Melmoth, trans. Quoted in Norman L. Geisler, *Baker's Encyclopedia of Christian Apologetics*. Grand Rapids: Baker Book House, 1998.

Ralls, Karen. *The Templars and the Grail*. Wheaton, IL: Theosophical Publishing House, 2003.

Ramm, Bernard. *Protestant Christian Evidences*. Chicago: Moody Press, 1953.

Ramsay, Sir W. M. *The Bearing of Recent Discovery on the Trustworthiness of the New Testament*. London: Hodder and Stoughton, 1915.

Ramsay, W. M. *St. Paul the Traveller and the Roman Citizen*. Grand Rapids: Baker Book House, 1962.

Richardson. "The Priory of Sion Hoax," *Gnosis: A Journey of the Western Inner Traditions* (Spring 1999).

Roberts, Alexander and James Donaldson, eds. *The Ante-Nicene Fathers*. Grand Rapids: Eerdmans, 1993.

Robertson, Archibald Thomas. *Word Pictures in the New Testament*. vols. I-V. Nashville: Broadman Press, 1930.

Robinson, James M. *The Nag Hammadi Library*. San Francisco: Harper SanFrancisco, 1978; 1990 ed.

Robinson, John A. T. *Redating the New Testament*. Philadelphia: Westminster, 1976.

Roper, Albert. *Did Jesus Rise from the Dead?* Grand Rapids: Zondervan Publishing House, 1965.

Sanders, C. *Introduction to Research in English Literary History*. New York: Macmillan Co., 1952.

Sanello, Frank. *The Knights Templar: God's Warriors and the Devil's Bankers*. Lanham, MD: Taylor, 2003.

Schaff, Philip. *History of the Christian Church*, Grand Rapids: Wm. B. Eerdmans, 1910.

—. *The Person of Christ*. New York: American Tract Society, 1913.

Schonfield, H. J. *The Passover Plot: New Light on the History of Jesus*. New York: Bantam, 1967.

Sherwin-White, A. N. *Roman Society and Roman Law in the New Testament*. Oxford: Clarendon Press, 1963.

Sherwin-White, A. N. *Roman Society and Roman Law in the New Testament*, reprint edition. Grand Rapids: Baker Book House, 1978.

Smith, Wilbur. *Therefore Stand*. Grand Rapids: Baker Book House, 1945.

Smith, William, ed. *Dictionary of Greek and Roman Antiquitie*, rev. ed. London: James Walton and John Murray, 1870.

Stoner, Peter W. *Science Speaks*. Chicago: Moody Press, 1963.

Strobel, Lee. *The Case for Christ*. Grand Rapids: Zondervan Publishing House, 1998.

—. *The Case for Easter*. Grand Rapids: Zondervan Publishing House, 1998.

Stott, John R. W. *Basic Christianity*. 2nd ed. Downers Grove, IL: InterVarsity Press, 1971.

Tacitus, Cornelius. *Annals*. In *Great Books of the Western World*, by Robert Maynard Hutchins, ed. vol. 15. Chicago: William Benton, 1952.

Tenney, Merrill C. The Reality of the Resurrection. Chicago: Moody Press, 1963.

Thorburn, Thomas James. *The Resurrection Narratives and Modern Criticism.* London: Kegan Paul, Trench, Trubner & Co., Ltd., 1910.

"Torch Run, Olympic Rings Not So Ancient," *The Herald-Mail.* July 14, 1996. (Accessed at www.herald-mail.com/news/1996/olympics/july14herald.html.)

Toynbee, Arnold. *Study of History.* vol. 6. London: Oxford University Press, 1947.

Unger, Merrill F. *Unger's Bible Dictionary.* rev. ed. Chicago: Moody Press, 1966.

Valiente, Doreen. *An ABC of Witchcraft Past & Present.* New York: St. Martin's Press, 1973.

Vanderkam, James, and Flint, Peter. *The Meaning of the Dead Sea Scrolls: Their Significance For Understanding the Bible, Judaism, Jesus, and Christianity.* San Francisco: Harper SanFrancisco, 2002.

Vermaseren, M. J. *Mithras: The Secret God.* London: Chatto and Windus, 1963.

Vos, Howard F., ed. *Can I Trust the Bible?* Chicago: Moody Press, 1963.

Walker, Williston. *A History of the Christian Church.* New York: Charles Scribner's Sons, 1970.

Walvoord, John F., and Roy B. Zuck, eds. *The Bible Knowledge Commentary: Old Testament.* Wheaton, IL: Victor Books, 1985.

Whedon, D. D. *Commentary of the Gospels Matthew–Mark.* vol. 9. New York: Hunt and Eaton, 1888.

Wilkins, Michael J., and J. P. Moreland, eds. *Jesus Under Fire: Modern Scholarship Reinvents the Historical Jesus.* Grand Rapids: Zondervan Publishing House, 1995.

William of Tyre. *Historia rerum in partibus transmarinis gestarum.*

Wurthwein, E. *The Text of the Old Testament: An Introduction to the Biblia Hebraica.* trans. by Erroll F. Rhodes. Grand Rapids: Eerdmans, 1979.

Yamauchi, Edwin M. *Pre-Christian Gnosticism.* 2nd ed. Grand Rapids: Baker Book House, 1983.

Zacharias, Ravi. *Can Man Live Without God?* Dallas: Word Publishing, 1994.

The Da Vinci Code: A Quest For Answers
by Josh McDowell

1. **Leaders Prepare with Over-arching Strategy**
— Read *The Last Christian Generation* in advance
— Understand how this generation has redefined Christianity
— Examine the 7 key principles for reclaiming a generation
— Act upon principles with Da Vinci Response Strategy

2. **Believers Equipped with Solid Answers**
— Launch 3-session small group study in conjunction with *Da Vinci Quest* book (applicable for youth and adults)
— Know answers to key questions raised by the movie

3. **Seekers Discover True Answers**
— Welcome discussions with seekers and skeptics by handing out mini-magazine, *Da Vinci Companion Guide*
— Take action. Believers share their *Da Vinci Quest* book with a seeker friend— a book that provides the true answers.

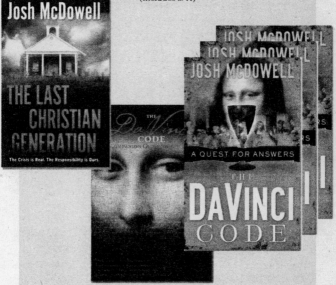

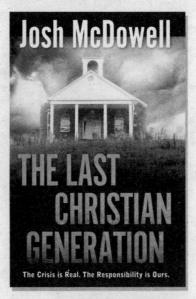